Dear Ms Mary,

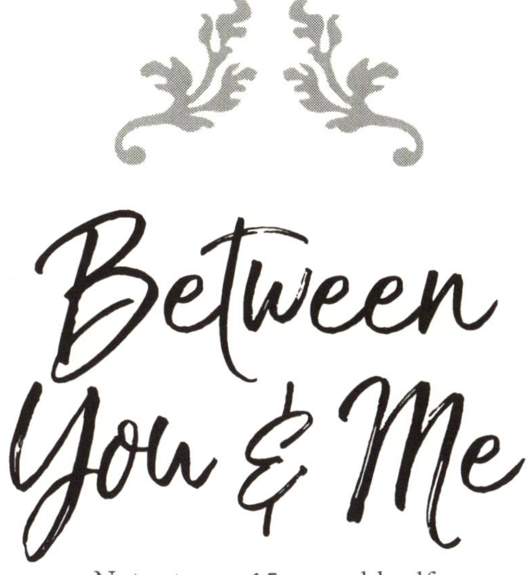

Notes to my 15 year old self
about life, growing up and the
power of spirituality

PRIYANKA CHATTERJEE

Thanks for your friendship, it means
more to me than I can tell
Wish you only the best
always...

Feb 23, 2024 Priyanka

First Edition

ISBN 978-0999301999

Designed by Jane Dixon Smith

To Ma & Baba,
Thank you for letting me fly

To Nitesh,
Thank you for being my enabler

& Nirvaan,
Thank you for reinforcing that Life is the greatest purpose

CONTENTS

INTRODUCTION

Do you feel a constant restlessness? Is there a nagging sadness always in the background? Do you feel like you've done everything you set out to do and there is still that void? That void that is impossibly hard to shrug off? It stays with you throughout the day no matter what. And you don't seem to have permission to let this secret out. You are either "too young" to feel these emotions or you "really need to focus on more important things" ... have you heard that from someone before? Do you feel utterly lost and, although you are going through the motions of life, you really need for this ride to stop because you are not enjoying this anymore? Does it sometimes feel like the greatest scam in the history of evolution – the fact that life ends with an anti-climax of sorts? Are you surprised how no one talks about this stuff, especially before depression arrives?

You are absolutely not alone and it's not a coincidence that you are reading this right now. I dealt with these demons for far too long in my teens and adult life and I feel incapable of not talking about them. This should be the most important discussion on the table – our youth is suffering and societal structures do not have any answers.

I had to find my answers myself through exploration and experience. There was no handbook or map handed down to me. I didn't even know what to ask for. The 15 year old Priyanka suffered in silence. And I know other 13, 14, 15 year olds are suffering today, and it only amplifies in their 20s. Questions become louder with no sight of the answers. It is an epidemic that no one seems to care about. We only see statistics about kids and teens suffering from depression and lament when they take the final steps of ending their life. No kid needs to die because the workings of life get overwhelming and they can't make sense of them. All we need is an honest discussion, a more public discussion without any judgment or stigma. That's all.

I wrote these notes to my 15 year old self when I hit my lowest. Everything on the outside was perfect but the depression was silently destroying me. These notes were conversations between her and me, intimate conversations to make it up to her, to wishfully think that I could travel back in time, hold her hand and be there for her. But talking to people across race, communities and the research of today proves that these notes may just be as relevant to other teens who are silently suffering and trying to make sense of it all.

There are no best practices around how to best read or use this book. These notes were written from a stream of consciousness and thus they don't follow any standard process. The quantity of words didn't matter: some conversations were long and some were more brief. When I was 'asked' to stop, I stopped. Read them as you wish, and if some words strike a chord, pause for a few seconds and close your eyes. I have also ended every note with a takeaway and a moment of contemplation. Feel free to write or think through these for a few seconds after reading the note. Writing your thoughts down forms a more solid platform for reflection, so I would encourage you to do this. Above all, use it as a friend. Because it's written by a friend who has been through most if not all of the things you are going through right now.

If my notes can help provide an answer or a new perspective on even one of the burgeoning questions in your mind, it will have served its purpose. And mine.

Much love,

Priyanka

ACKNOWLEDGEMENTS

I wish to acknowledge my parents for wishing for a better life for me and creating possibilities that have allowed me to gain perspectives that I deeply value. I am also grateful for my husband Nitesh: our decades of companionship have brought indelible peace into my life. A big kiss to my newborn, Nirvaan, who has been a personification of the blissful liberation of spirit since the day he arrived.

I would like to take this opportunity to two incredible teachers from my formative years, Mrs. Z. Reena Charan and Mr. Anup Chakraborty, who made this small town girl believe she could do more than her limited mind allowed her to imagine. Their little votes of confidence from many years ago can be found in the pages of this book.

But most of all, I am thankful to the source within me that knocked on my door time and again when I got complacent and pushed me to keep writing. I am grateful for this life that has afforded me so many experiences and perspectives.

I. GOING BEYOND

"I am slowly starting to drift away"

"Drift where?"

"Somewhere else …"

The Beginning of the Journey

On this path effort never goes to waste, and there is no failure.

Even a little effort towards spiritual awareness will protect you from the greatest fear.

~The Bhagavad Gita (2:40)

Dear P,

The vagaries of life are splendid. There are numerous people to please, expectations to be met, successes to be had, money to be earned, houses to be built and the latest cars to be bought. The Gita calls it *Leela* and its splendor is no less than a grand opera. The more twists and turns, the more emotions it conjures, the more interesting the show is for the audience. We are so engrossed that the awareness of our own participation in the show eludes us. That's what makes the show of life such an interesting subject to consider and introspect on.

There will come a point, a fork in the road, where we either decide to stay in the game as a participant or venture outside and instead stay in the game as an observer.

So why did I venture outside of the show? Because I was not having fun anymore. In many respects, I lived my life by the book. The definitions of success were clear, some defined by family but mostly by society. The toil and hard work for a better future was the only thing that drove me. Ideals of heroes from the past and the future, some famous and some not, were put forth for me to meet. At every milestone I was made to believe that life would only get better once I reached the next milestone. I kept up with it, living only for a better future. The present had minuscule value, if any. Living through every day in a hazy stupor was not a lot of fun and I couldn't wait to meet the future of my dreams. More importantly, I couldn't wait to be *happy* ... in the future.

At the age of 27, I had met most expectations, lived up to most ideals, and possessed things that would define me as successful. There was everything! I expected to be blown away with peace and happiness, to feel so complete that I did not need anything else, to feel the lightness in my body I hadn't felt for years, to laugh often and experience not having any expectations. *I felt none of that.* In fact, I felt a *void*, a physical sense of hollowness.

For a few months, I questioned often, "Is this it?" "Is this really it?" The cycle of earning and buying was getting boring, and that was the only definition of success I knew: when you earn more, you buy more and more things make you happy. *This cycle was not working for me anymore.* It was almost like I stepped off of a high speed treadmill and I couldn't get back on. I had many questions, and answers didn't seem to be available. I looked around – my parents, friends, and relatives – would they know? Alas ... they didn't seem to, and I was too scared to probe further.

A voice inside advised that there is *something more*. Something more I needed to do. I also had a vague understanding that this 'more' was infinitely important to discover, more important than anything that I had ever done or would ever do. That's all I got for a year and a half.

I functioned in a stupor during this time, having immense trouble relating to my family, friends and co-workers. My job seemed particularly mechanical because I saw it as a claimed prize that did nothing to get me closer to the answers I was seeking. My work throughput was not a priority at all.

The heaviness in my heart and more importantly the urgency I felt inside was so strong that it would often make me cry. I remember very distinctly the day I folded my hands in front of, well... the air in my room. The only things I could utter were, "I surrender to you. Please show me the way. Point me to answers." I surrendered because I couldn't see a way out.

Soon after, during a commonplace online browsing session, I stumbled upon a video of Eckhart Tolle explaining silence. I didn't know what to make of it but I recognized a truth in his words. One video led to another and soon I was devouring books by the day. Eckhart Tolle, Marianne Williamson, Shri Ramana Maharishi, Neale Donald Walsh, the Dalai Lama became my friends and I listened to every You Tube video I could find of them. They didn't lead me to answers, but they started pointing in the same direction. The fact that there are other people seeking the same truth made me a part of a universal community. I was not stupid or loony anymore. I was not alone

There was a strange reassurance that I was being ushered, into *something*. After two years of seeking answers, I was finally getting somewhere. There was a certain lightness, an understanding that I was right to believe that there is a higher truth, that there is this whole realm of awesomeness inside of us that's ready to be discovered.

It gave me a new perspective, and I started reviewing my entire teenage and adolescence with this new-found wisdom. This new dimension of awareness helped me analyze certain poignant situations in my life. A certain part of me was angry that no one guided me, they just led me on. I felt distraught that I had led a very ego-based life till now and that society just helped strengthen it. I started writing notes to my 15 year old self about my everyday realizations. This would be my way of making up for not being there for her when she needed this wisdom.

Takeaway

Don't get me wrong, I am no more enlightened than the next person. In fact I still struggle with the web of predefined mind patterns that continue to surface throughout the day. Each day is a challenge and an opportunity to convert a pattern and have a better relationship with my thoughts. It doesn't help that this journey is one of great solitude. You won't find many friends and family who can relate to you at this level (if and when you find them, keep them!). Needless to say, there is still much to discover. I am on a journey into myself. The destination is unknown and I strongly feel it doesn't exist. But I have developed an awareness that is worth nurturing. This small awareness within us has the power to change mankind. We are reaching a time in history where human extinction due to wars and climatic changes seems impending. We cannot change the course of history but we can all rise up to the occasion and kindle a deeper awareness of who we really are – that is the only way we can save ourselves from, well, ourselves.

Moment of contemplation:

Do you feel a constant emptiness inside? Almost like a humming sound? Think through your current feelings and feel free to find analogies to express them. For example, I mostly felt a nagging but very mild depression from the age of 13 to 27 and a constant discomfort at the pit of my stomach.

Have you been searching for an answer or have you not started looking just yet? (P.S. We are all in different phases of seeking and exploration.)

____

____

____

____

"It's like I know what is right, but something, something strong, drives me towards what is not."

"What is it?"

"I wish I knew"

An Epidemic Called Ego

"What would the ego do without a 'problem'?"

~Michael Jefferys

Dear P,

The hardest thing is to know in our heart that something is really true, really, really true, but not be able to pursue it or know it fully because of a mental aberration in our belief translated into our behavior. Nothing else in the world, in my opinion, kills the day like ego.

My ego was very active from the get go. I had a strong picture of who I should be and what I should have in life to be happy. I was deeply clear on the things that people could or could not attempt with me. I didn't enjoy other people's success as much as my own and felt beat easily if my over achieving qualities did not result in glory. I was most competitive with my closest friends and sometimes it dawned on me that I was friends with them to ensure I knew them well enough to beat them. Needless to say, I was often overcome by sadness and despair, because someone was always better than me at something. Part of me wanted to be happy for others and do all the other righteous things, but it always lost.

I don't know when my ego developed. Maybe it was when I figured out how to deceive my mother to get that extra scoop of ice-cream, or realizing where I and my brother stand in my parent's love index. It may have been formed from observing my interactions in my social circle and their consequences. Competition may have been a big reason. Because I really felt I had to fight against everything else to justify or honor the picture I created in my childhood – the picture of being the best. And that meant I had to be different, I had to be 'more' than others. Separation yielded a loss of love, a distinction, a difference. Now my ego was full-blown. It had become a self-fulfilling system!

I understood ego very differently in the past than how I understand it now (there is absolutely nothing wrong in that. That's why we have life – to continuously update our definitions, as long as we update it ourselves, based on our own experiences). I thought ego was something you have when you are full of yourself. It was fairly common to call someone out as egotistical when they were acting like a jackass. Ego had a negative connotation, of course, but it was an attribute that a man possessed, not a separate entity. That was my long-winded definition.

Here is what I know now. Ego is a well-funded, self-sufficient, strategic, organically growing energy organism that is an alternative personality of us. Every time we are not present, that is we are not in touch with who we really are, we are in touch with our ego. The ego is constantly looking for you to break your vow and come live in the unconscious. That's ego's dreamland. An unconscious being is the ultimate container that provides safe housing and entertainment for the ego. As it moves through the container, it is amused by what it is able to make us say, do and feel. It is the powerful mafia which is constantly looking out for its survival and expansion of territory.

The last thing it wants you to do is to connect with your inner self and show it the door.

It is also very skillful. You can see the impact when you meditate. Think of all the incessant thoughts while meditating, most of them against the act of meditation. It tries to dissuade me incessantly from being in meditation every day. "*What are you even doing?*" "*I know who told you about this. She is a complete fad lover,*" "*You will never improve doing this!*" Somewhere in the journey of the million thought conversations, ego became the master and I the slave. It is hypocritical, doesn't want you to have friends, has an excessive comparison syndrome where you always underperform and others are always bad, and does not want you to improve at anything: it's fueled when we falter or make the slightest of mistakes – it's just a total mess and makes our lives one, too!

Oh, and it loves drama! Any kind of drama! Someone said something curt in a fit, someone did something against our wish, our partner did not comply with our rules – it just needs something to latch on to. It's the leech that sticks and then keeps sucking. Once it latches on, it can keep spinning our head on the same topic over days, weeks and months. There are multiple drama offshoots that spring out – "*he always does this, remember that time! This marriage is not going anywhere!*"

I wonder about the countless divorces, breakups and loss of friendships caused by this monster, which truly is an epidemic. When a disease is widespread, we call it an emergency situation. We are living in a constant state of emergency because of ego – it's just that nobody's there to call it out. It is silently rocking our world and we don't even know it. We blame the spouse, the parent, the friend – it's the ego. Our own ego. Their ego. The funny thing is that when relationships break, it's not the two people communicating with each other as their authentic selves; there is no existence of presence. It's just egos butting heads against each other, all the while refueling and recharging each other. And when everything is over and done, we are left with a deep sense of loss but the ego does the upkeep on the pride factor. Every time we feel the need to apologize, the ego says, "Shhh, not needed!" Love is the greatest victim of the war of egos. And we blame destiny, luck and, of course, God.

The only way I have known to oust ego from my life is to not give it free shelter every day. Every negative emotion, whether it's anger, jealousy, boredom, the need to complain or despair, arises from the fact that ego is hanging around in my house. So, whenever I see any of them rising within me, I holler, "Hey there, ego. I know it's you! Now get the hell out." It resists, provides excuses and then reluctantly leaves, promising to come back when it sees even the smallest crack in the door.

Sometimes, I am not that strong and I give in. And I feel all the emotions that I don't want to feel, all the while knowing what's at play, but I just don't have enough fire power to drive it out. Then I just observe it, live it and let the time pass. And there are times when I am connected to myself at a different level because of my meditation practice, writing and self-awareness. In these times, ego does not even try. Above all, when it comes to the prized relationships in my life, I hire a fierce watchman outside the door. I have realized our relationships need to be vehemently protected from ego: ours and others'.

We will always have something appending the I AM: that's the fun of being in the physical world. I AM a homeowner, I AM a writer, I AM a meditator, I AM a car owner, I AM a daughter, I AM a wife – our world is made to operate in the realms of I AM … X (it doesn't matter what this is). Our identity and our ownerships define our relationship to others and society at large. The issue arises when we are at a loss in the event of a strain in any of the appendices of I AM. What if I lose my home, my car, my ability to write, my ability to meditate, if my marriage has issues or there is tension with my parents – we break apart. This is where the ego indulges in a celebration. It loves that humans are so attached to names and various physical identities. It is constantly playing games with those identities via our incessant thoughts. And when it successfully breaks that association of the I AM and X, it throws a party. It won. Because we as humans don't think the remnant I AM is of any value to us, since we didn't spend any time understanding or empowering it. The X was all that mattered, and when that has gone, all hell has broken loose.

I have heard that masters have no ego. That would be something. It would be liberating to say the least. But I am not there yet. My ego creeps up every so often. But it knows I know it by name and that I am not letting it have a free ride anymore. It also knows that in addition to putting up a good fight, I also know how to send it to rehab for a long time. It is simply me being connected to I AM, just I AM. Realizing that I AM is where we are home, where ego does not reside. It is our *aham*, our self-awareness of how divine we are.

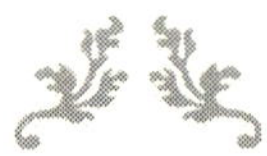

Takeaway

Ego is an extremely vulnerable, homeless thing. Homelessness is not ego's comfort zone. Its survival depends on latching on to a home. And it wants to remain under the hood: the more conspicuous it is, the weaker it gets. So, let's beam some divine light on ego, our very own light and strive to dissolve any traces of it in our system. Let's recognize the intruder the moment it steps into our sacred space. It doesn't belong here anymore. In fact, it can't even enter the building, let alone the room. This space is ours only. The truest, most sacred part of us resides there and it is perfectly fine without a roommate.

Moment of contemplation:

Who would you be if you were stripped off of all your titles and responsibilities?

Are you aware of your ego rising? How is your ego-self different from you?

Think of a relationship in your life that is suffering because of egos on one or both sides. What can you do differently?

"I feel hollow sometimes."

"I know you do."

"What does it mean?"

"You know exactly what it means."

Feeling of Hollowness

"Let yourself be silently drawn by the stronger pull of what you really love."

~ Jalaluddin Rumi

Dear P,

Oh that hollow feeling! I felt there was a hole in my heart. There was a physical hollowness in life that had become a part of my life. It felt like a fish put out of water trying to wring the life out of itself as it just couldn't take life anymore. I felt angry and irritable for no apparent reason. I just wouldn't feel good. This feeling took over my body day and night. I would wake up at strange hours like I was supposed to do something, but I wouldn't have a clue what to do. For the longest time, 3:47AM was my time to wake up, fidget and then put myself back to sleep. Then I had the whole freakin' day to get through! I would carry this remorse like I was living a lie every day – meeting friends, playing games, etc., was fun, but the feeling remained in the background. My hollowness became my companion during my teens. I romanced it and almost felt privileged because of its presence, like I was special. The ego can do really strange things sometimes.

For the longest time I thought I was depressed. There was a constant feeling of lack. But I just couldn't shift the heaviness and boredom I felt constantly. I had everything going for me. A house, car, a six-figure salary. But I was bored and had no joy. There is stigma attached to saying you don't have joy when you have every material thing in life. *How could you not have joy? Such an ungrateful woman!* You can hear the voices in your head. They don't go away.

Money was a portal to unknown happiness in my belief system. That did not go that far. I just knew that earning tons of money would open up a world for me where I could be whatever, do whatever and live the life of my dreams. I could do a lot of things with my money – travel, eat good food, shop. After the honeymoon period – the six months of buying everything under the sun, I found myself sitting on my couch and thinking two things: all this meant nothing to me and I was ready to buy more. Material wealth and external things are tricky friends. They are needy and while they give you company sometimes, they leave you feeling unfulfilled. You could buy the most expensive house in town, but it soon appears unworthy and the idea that something better is out there will haunt you soon after. I couldn't find the friend in my salary that I was always brought up to believe I would.

I had to look outside the material. Question why I was feeling this way. What was going on in my life that was causing me to question its worthiness? Was I too comfortable? Was I not doing the job that I was meant to? Did I know what it was? No, I didn't. I just knew it was not of this world, and I knew it was a communication with something larger. Could I prove it? No. But I felt it in my bones.

Hollowness is our true north or may be more accurately, it's the gravitational pull toward our true north while we are away doing important things or apparently important things. Hollowness, discomfort, restlessness – these are all pointers to our greatest truth. They compel us to pay heed to what we have forgotten about why we are here. Life wants us to live an aligned life, where there is no effort and no resistance.

I realized I was being required to make a life change. For me, it was to go back to the source and just be grateful and be present in my doings. Go back to writing. I was supposed to write and I was not writing, at all. Life had taken over. The chores of life were taking me away from my true calling of writing the book I was supposed to write. But I was not manifesting that calling because of inertia or a hundred other reasons.

If you are feeling the jitters, it is time to make a change. Most times, it is an urgent knock to go back to what you know you have to do. For me, it was prioritizing writing over the 'important things' I was doing every day. More often than not, it's right in front of our eyes and something we are aware of. The trick is to confront the lies that we tell ourselves. I was lying about my schedule and the things I had to do. The truth was, I was creating these chores so I didn't have to write. Not because I didn't love writing: I was rebelling against the discipline of writing.

Takeaway

Whatever you do, do not ignore this feeling. It will drive you crazy. Nuts. Bonkers. Have a conversation with yourself rather than shoving this under the carpet. Pay heed to what it's pointing to. You will be thankful for it – both for the cloud of hollowness to finally leave you and also the miraculous changes that paying heed to our discontent brings into our life. Do. Not. Ignore It.

Moment of contemplation:

Do you feel a constant sense of lack and sadness? What does it feel like?

If you have to be honest with yourself right now, what is that one thing this you are being asked to look at?

____

____

____

____

"Let's talk about your thoughts today. Have you given them any thought?"

"I have a lot of thoughts, mostly relentless. But I guess that's just me talking."

Decoding our Thoughts

"The single most vital step on your journey towards enlightenment is this: learn to dis-identify from your mind, the light of your consciousness grows stronger."

~Eckhart Tolle

Dear P,

As a teen and much later into my 20s, I did not think my thoughts to be any different than who I was. My thoughts were me and vice versa. They were constant, relentless and gained momentum without doing much. We romanticize thinkers, and for the longest time, I took pride in my thinking. I was sad through most of my teens. I never knew why. I know now.

If I could verbalize all the thoughts I have in a day, I can safely say I would not be out in society. But back then, I never verbalized them; instead I internalized my thoughts. This internalization led to sadness (which I could not speak of) and a sense of loneliness (which I could not express). My thoughts talked down to me endlessly and I believed them because here is a voice talking directly into my head. Since everyone seemed to be going through the same experience, I assumed there was nothing abnormal.

I believe the single biggest reason for human insanity is not letting go of our conditioning to allow thoughts to go rogue. Just close your eyes and sit quietly for a minute. Just a minute. One thought comes, picks up the pieces of another thought and BAM, there is another thought. It floats into your past, the future, hardly ever stopping in the present. Soon, the minute has distressed you to such an extent that you don't want to close your eyes again. That's why meditation has a stigma attached to it. Closing of the eyes is synonymous with hammering thoughts. This experience also gives you a peek into how incessant thoughts are in our lives and how much of an everyday companion this illusory thing is. It speaks constantly and mostly from a negative space.

We are not our thoughts. We have thoughts. With practice, we can have full control of our thoughts. But we don't know that. Let's do this quick exercise. At this moment right now, imagine that your mind, which is churning all the thoughts, has a switch and you are turning it off with clear authority. Get into a no-thought state. It will not last long, may be only a second or two, but experience it while it lasts. In that moment, you could have potentially experienced the most peace and tranquility that you have experienced the entire day, week or month. That's the power of a still mind, a no-thought mind. The journey is to stop the identification of the mind with the self. Enlightenment is finding that permanent off switch!

In our daily lives, we rarely quieten up. We are going at it, and some. Alcohol and drugs give us a glimpse of that state of stillness but they come with their own baggage. That's why people go back to get some more. But these are artificial ways of experiencing transcendence which also harm the body tremendously.

There are way less harmless techniques to slow them down. I find breathing to be the easiest method to experience stillness. Breathe deeply through your nose and ensure you are breathing into your belly and not your chest. Now hold the breath for three counts and then gently release through your mouth. Right after you breathe out, be in that serene space for a few seconds. Repeat three more times or more as you are guided. This short but surprisingly powerful tool fills us up with so much clarity.

Another exercise that has greatly helped me come out of the unconscious stream of thinking is to watch the thinker. I learnt this from *The Power of Now* by Eckhart Tolle. When the stream of thinking begins, become attentive and observe the entity generating the thoughts. Do not identify with it. Just watch it. The watcher is a higher consciousness that has arisen because of the simple decision to watch your thoughts. Soon, you will be laughing at some of the funny stuff our thoughts make up.

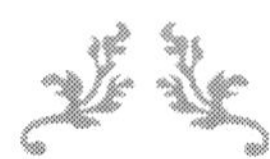

Takeaway

The bottom line is to give ourselves a break from the constant chatter. I don't think about getting rid of it. It would be unrealistic given the kind of lives we live. But the small gaps of no-thinking we create throughout the day can be a game changer and boost us in far greater ways than we would think. They also have a way to multiply with practice. Play with the gaps. Dis-identify from thoughts. Reclaim yourself.

Moment of contemplation:

Close your eyes for a minute. Do you see a pattern in the thoughts that arise?

Write down your experience after doing the "watch the thinker" exercise above. Were you able to completely see the thinker as a separate entity or was there a partial overlap?

____

____

____

____

"How are you?"

"Fine. But why does this feel so heavy?"

The D Word

"I don't think people understand how stressful it is to explain what's going on inside your head when you don't even understand it yourself."

~ Anonymous

Dear P,

I know you are sad. On most days, sadness takes over your life, holding your smile hostage. You don't feel like participating in friendly banter or anything else that would cause your sadness to feel less than important. It has taken over your life. Day turns into night, days turn into months and years, but the shadow remains. Where do you go from here? Is this how life is going to be forever? The world can give it any name it wants and add as much stigma as it pleases: the fact remains that depression is a real thing. Life sucks right now. You can't explain it, people closest to you don't understand it, it's getting worse with every passing day and there is no help in sight.

All I ever wanted from the world was a, *"Hello, how are you? Are you doing alright? You can talk to me anytime."* I just wanted to talk to someone. Anyone. No one had the time to listen and I didn't have the courage to talk. When I mustered some up, I received a barrage of judgments. I shut up. Self-confidence was at an all-time low. The truth is, depression had made me very weak. I just felt weak everywhere – from my mind to my toenails. I only needed a nudge to fall down on my knees, just like I probably needed just one honest conversation to get me back up.

I remember being taken to the doctor because of my anxiety issues. The doctor asked me what was really happening. I just bawled and continued to cry for the next twenty minutes. The doctor and my parents seemed perplexed. He gave me some meds which I never remember taking. But I clearly remember the day because I cried profusely in front of a complete stranger in response to *"How are things?"* That was my state of mind. The tears had become too heavy to not fall.

What is depression to me? It's an unfortunate condition of the human mind which arises when a person goes unsupported, from their parents, their friends and social structures. It's a minion that gets the stage because everyone else bailed and it's now suddenly popular and powerful. It's the benign tumor that turns malignant due to lack of care. All it needs is one shoulder to lean one, just one that cares, and cares at the right time. Once that catches it before it can spew venom everywhere.

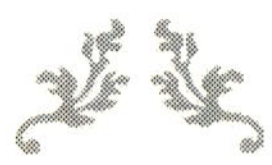

Takeaway

What am I to say to you? You have been so brave through all this. Trying your best to protect the fort. Two things that saved me: meditation and writing. Find that place where meditation is taught or a group of people come together to connect. Write your thoughts down. If that's hard for you, talk it out on the phone. The idea is take this thing out of your body, placing it on a paper or on a recording device, and then letting the alignment from a simple meditation practice replace it with your own energy, which is pure and safe. But its just so hard to do it all alone, so hard. You strive so hard to pick yourself up, and one thought, just one repeating thought triggered by a person or a situation brings it back to ground zero. Here is where our parents can be rescuers, if only they can rise above their own ego patterns and really notice what's going on with their son or daughter. The signs are all there, you only need to stop ignoring them or living in denial. So dear parent, here is my plea:

Recognize it, please. She is sad. You know she is sad. And it's not because children nowadays are sad, spoilt and have a perpetual attitude. The world seems gloomy to her, despite the joys you have brought to her life. She doesn't have anything in her arsenal to fight this thing: this is a downward spiral she is unable to control. She feels cornered. She feels alone. Please catch her before she falls too deep. Take her for a walk and talk – ask her not just for her grades but also the state of her emotions, no matter how taboo you feel that is for your family. Just let her lean on you. Encourage her to meditate and teach her skills and tools to combat the mental chatter which is pushing her to believe that life is not worth living.

Depression is not bigger than a supportive and loving home. It's the lack of it that permits depression to step in to a home. Guard your home. Just like you have a security sticker in your yards, put up a "Depression, stay the F* out" sticker." Fight for your kids. Fight for them, please.

Moment of contemplation:

If this note resonates with you, can you write down how you have been feeling?

What kind of help from others would be healing to you?

Can you take the step today to speak to someone close about your feeling?

"Let's talk about the knot today, shall we?"

"There is nothing to say, it's just always there."

Fear is Inevitable

"Fear is inevitable, I have to accept that,
but I cannot allow it to paralyze me."

~Isabel Allende

Dear P,

I wake up with the knot in the pit of my stomach, yet again. For as long as I can remember, I have carried this intangible lump inside me. It has gone with me everywhere. It is a very physical thing, I sometimes compare it to a person living inside me.

I am fairly certain it woke up with me and there was a small span of time when I was in the deepest of sleeps when it took a break and went out for a walk. Terrified – that's how I felt all the time. Muscles taut and butterflies in the stomach…I was a wreck, ready for a meltdown anytime. It was many years later that I could put a name to it.

It was fear.

As a child, I was a riot. Fearless, bold, crazy, wild – I manifested and personified all of those qualities. I would pick up a street puppy without flinching, sing with gusto, laugh uncontrollably, and dance like there was no one in the room. There was a charisma in everything and with that an underlying serenity. As a child, I saw no differences between people – it was just natural to treat everyone the same way, irrespective of their race, creed, color, position, intelligence or appearance.

Then something happened – growing up happened, and it was not the same anymore. It planted the seeds for fear that engulfed me in every respect. Growing up included learning the dos and don'ts, right and wrong. *Don't touch this, don't giggle in front of people, be diplomatic, dance with some reservations, don't talk to strangers, don't aspire for money, and do earn a lot of money.* The propriety list was set in my cache memory for easy reference in every situation.

By the time my teens arrived, I was more aware of the *don't than the dos*. We don't realize this naturally, but significant energy is required to maintain the lists. And then the quick check of the appropriate response for every situation – that needs energy, too. Soon, social gatherings either become a breeze because you have mastered the art of managing the list or you just don't socialize.

By thirteen, I was physically tensed all the time. My muscles were taut with many butterflies in my stomach. *Is it daylight or dark out, is that man following me? Will the right words come out of my mouth? What if my answer does not please them? This may not be the right thing to do* – soon I would find myself better off in my room with a book than facing a crowd.

Fear causes us to constantly judge ourselves against the world. And it ensures we always, always do worse than our potential. It will pretend to be your best ally, but its agenda is not to explore the best in you. Its purpose is to cripple you to such an extent that you don't experience true freedom anymore. Not surprisingly, some of the lowest points in my life have come from moments where I was engulfed in raw fear. Suddenly this very charismatic girl who loved and laughed found the world to be an utterly dark and gloomy place. *A place she is not worthy of. A place she is not good enough for.* The world had not changed; my lens was so dense with fear that my view of the world took a downward spiral.

Through my teens and 20s, I tried to cope with fear of different kinds – fear of public speaking, fear of authority in school and at work, fear of displeasing someone, fear of saying NO, fear of not being loved or appreciated, fear of my own shortcomings and their implications for my life, the list was very long and I couldn't articulate it then, which made life much harder.

Recognition of a problem is always the first step and it was eluding me. Fear confused me because I could never point it out by its name. We are not taught how to recognize and deal with fear in schools or in other forms of our childhood education and upbringing. It was merely a *physically uncomfortable feeling*. "*One day I will figure out what the hell this is,*" that's all I could muster at that time.

Fear defined me. Omnipresent and overpowering, I was aware of its presence constantly. Fear played me and I stood there with my arms wide open in complete surrender. With no tools in my arsenal to protect myself, my vulnerability was the only thing that was mine.

I never assumed I could reach out for help, either. The idea of approaching my parents with a, "*Mom, Dad – I suffer from great fear... fear of everything*"...nah! And coming out to friends would make me look weak or not good enough. Not happening! I often wondered if other people were facing anything similar or if it was just me. It isolated me in a corner.

Then one day, I stood up from the corner. I just stood up. Fear had consumed far too much of my time on the planet and I was tired, tired of running from it. And frankly, I didn't know what else to do.

I started reading books on fear, watching any video I could find on the Internet on the topic and journaling my feelings. Devouring every piece of information I could find on the subject, I was ready to defeat it. Surprisingly, I started the process of 'understanding' fear instead.

And then came the aha moment – the realization that I don't need to protect myself from it, I just need to accept its existence and then let go. The fact that it was a universal phenomenon and that everybody including the most successful people in the world suffer from fear comforted me. I was not the only one after all. The best solution to any problem is to get clarity on it. To get to know it so well that it doesn't seem like a stranger anymore. When fear came in, I knew it was normal to feel it and the question then was – what am I going to do with it?

Fear hasn't left me yet. It drops by every chance it gets. But fear is 'fear' now. Fear is like the 'nervousness,' 'anger,' 'unease' of the world for me. Rather than being an enemy, it's now a sticky friend who needs to be skillfully managed.

Fear will *never* not be there, just like different experiences that still bring about the same gamut of emotions in us. Fear is largely based on the truths we have told or want to tell ourselves. It's a direct outcome of historic data in our minds, making millions of permutations and combinations of stories that may have nothing to do with our lives.

One step that really helped in my journey was to ask myself the underlying truth every time I experienced fear. 100%, yes 100% of the time, I realized I completely made it up. I MADE UP MOST OF MY TRUTHS.

Slowly and steadily, I started changing the building blocks in my mind. For example, if I don't say my yes to my boss for one more piece of work, *he will not shoot me*! Or If I say no to my friend's invitation, *she will not hate me forever* (and even if she does, what's the underlying truth there?). These things are just not factual or realistic: they're at best hypothetical. The trick is to be honest about the underlying data we harbor. Once that cat is out of the bag, fear is vulnerable.

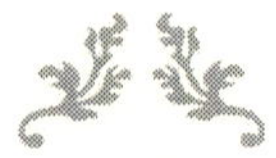

Takeaway

The first big win was to recognize fear as a separate entity than me. Fear rejoices in that fact that it diminishes us to a point that it's hard to see ourselves without that feeling. We become fear. Stepping out from that circle helps us with objectivity, which is precious in these situations.

The second win came with accepting fear. Know that fear will always try to sneak in. That's just what it does. How we establish the protocols of the relationship is in our hands.

It helps to study our fear too. Really study it. *What are you feeling? What is fear threatening you with this time? Is it really true that this can happen? If it does happen, what will it really do to you?* Can you deal with what will happen?

Connecting with our soul will always help keep us centered and grounded. All fear finds its genesis in the risk of losing our lives. When we are really connected to our soul, we realize how formless and indestructible our true selves are. And that sets us free. How do we connect with our soul? – Silence, prayer and meditation are three tools that I bring into my days as much as I can. They help me ground and bring alignment into my life

Last but not least, be amused. Be amused at fear's existence and the heaviness it brings to our lives, out of events that may be insignificant in the bigger scheme of things. Being late to a meeting, an uncomfortable conversation, failure of all kinds – they are never really as catastrophic as we make them out to be.

Constant reflection on a more balanced perspective will guide us through those trying times when fear gets the better of us and we are left with the 'physically uncomfortable feeling.' Let's understand fear better and let it amuse us … life is too short and too beautiful to give in.

Fear will always be there, but it can be tamed. Manage it. Manage it every day until your practice intuitively curbs it from raising its head in your everyday life.

Moment of contemplation:

How does fear manifest in your life? Write down the exact physical sensations in your body and the time of the day it's most active.

Which activities or events trigger the most fear in you?

How has fear impacted your quality of life? Think of a few activities you have given up on because of the anxiety around them.

____

____

____

____

"So, I just signed up to speak at this thing."

"And?"

"I feel like I've made the biggest mistake."

Life's Big Moments

"F-E-A-R has two meanings: 'Forget Everything and Run' or 'Face Everything and Rise.' The choice is yours."

~Zig Ziglar

Dear P,

You know those moments, when you took on a very big project and now have to deliver, that presentation in front of the bigwigs, the speech that somehow magically has to come out of your mouth extempore and countless other such moments. Your hands are sweaty, the butterflies are just going berserk, your heart beats so fast that you can actually feel it, and in the midst of it you wonder, *why did I take this on?*

I was thirteen and quite the popular kid in school but I avoided any situation that would open me up to public scrutiny. I took the easy route. Then one day I decided to prove a point to myself and volunteered to speak extempore on a topic from a fish bowl (*what got into me?!?).*

There I was in front of the entire school, may be 4,000 kids. The topic that day is still fresh in my memory – "the rising cost of living". I had a minute to get my thoughts together and then was given the microphone. I barely spoke two sentences. Then there was an awkward silence for two long minutes that still sends shivers through my spine. I cried for three straight days. It changed me somewhere deep.

Fast forward seventeen years: I volunteered to participate at an idea competition at my company. It was a ten minute presentation battle to present a revolutionary idea in front of the entire office. I didn't sleep for two days, as the memory of that day in school rattled me. I sent an email to my manager saying that I wouldn't be able to do it for personal reasons. The next day I felt awful. I felt like I had defeated myself without getting onto the battlefield, which is worse than losing. The inside of me suddenly became vocal and decided to speak up. *Life is about living, not giving up before losing. Life is a canvas and I am not painting because the canvas will get dirty – what fun is in that?* I couldn't stay put anymore. I got back to my manager, delighting him with the news as I got him out of the misery of looking for a replacement.

The next day I prepped for it as if I was in front of a live audience. I repeated to myself:

1. *Life is about experience*
2. *Be yourself*
3. *You will be alright no matter what*

But life situations are never handed over to you without some show time and drama. The opposite team had an excellent presentation with audio/visual and exciting props. I was nervous, as my presentation was not fun but more of an approach and included an executable plan. I did not have props. The only audio/visual I had was *me*. At that moment, I repeated the three bullet points to myself again and again. I decided to live that moment fully and bring myself into it as much as I can, not my ego who wants to look good but more of who I really am when I am not bothered what people think of me. I amazed myself! I had the room in fits of laughter. In fact, I didn't even know how I conjured up those one- liners at the moment. I aced the presentation. This was a different memory than the first.

I contemplated on this the next day and juxtaposed the two experiences. Yes, there was the difference in experience and maturity. But I know I could have spoken on that topic at thirteen. It was a very similar setting and situation. Only this time, I did something very different. *I allowed my true self to shine through.* I didn't let my thoughts start their tirade. I didn't permit my ego to hang me dry again.

I pondered over why we take these moments on. Something inside of us calls us to do so.

We take it on because life wants to live itself. It's the ego that makes us feel that we bit more than we can chew. Where we will be in the next 15 years, or when we are 85, largely depends on these very moments. We are the culmination of all of the moments where we were scared to death and rose above it nevertheless. Yes it's not easy. It's freaking scary. It's scary because we are denting a wall within us. The shackles and chains that create the drama and stories of our lives don't want us to break all the barriers.

Fear is ego's defense mechanism to keep us where we are. But when we stand up to it, something very magical transpires. Ego transmutes into an appreciative opponent. Our ego is the master of its work, so when we the immortal warrior stand up to our mortal personality, the ego applauds and steps out. That's why there is always this tipping point to these moments of great fear, *after which there is great peace.*

Takeaway

These transcendental opportunities are always around us. We need only take notice. But we try to drown them in everyday noise, sometimes even deliberately. If we were to look at our lives right now, there absolutely have to be at least three such opportunities that are staring at us to take them on. Take them on, I say. Take them on. If you are scared taking something on, that is the right direction. This is the only way to evolve. Soon enough you realize, your picture of it was far scarier than it ever actually turns out to be. Almost every single time.

Moment of contemplation:

Think about a project, at work or in your personal life that you did not take on because you were too scared. Also indicate what you thought would happen if things went wrong.

Now list the positive consequences that could have taken place if you did take them on.

Are there projects in your life at work or home that are looking for you to take them on? Prioritize them in the order of enjoyment and list them here.

Think about the reasons why you are avoiding these projects and your worst case scenario for each.

"I hate sitting by myself."

"Why?"

"It's almost like my head explodes when things are silent."

Listen to the Silence

"All man's miseries derive from not being able to sit quietly in a room alone."

~Blaise Pascal

Dear P,

As a teen, I would be constantly restless with energy that wanted to transform itself into something meaningful but didn't really know where to go. It kept swirling inside me like a twister. This feeling would amplify whenever I found myself alone, devoid of distractions with some semblance of silence. So, I did the best thing I could: *run away into a crowd.* I started running away from any situation that could potentially involve silence and arduously tried to never be alone. The goal was to always be doing something: watching movies, going on random dates, dinners or just hanging out with friends. I dreaded going back to my room, where silence would manifest itself. It was almost like it had something to say to me, but I did not want to hear it. I was running hard.

Then one day, it happened. I found myself at a quaint bookstore reading a book and in between sipping on my coffee and flipping to the next page, *I introduced myself to silence.* It was cordial. It just said hello and that it was happy to finally meet me. And then it did something unexpected – it said *goodbye for now. You can always come to this spot whenever you feel like.* After that, the twister was not as strong anymore. Silence had liberated my fearful mind from itself. And I started visiting it more often.

Silence is complex in nature and yet so simple. Disliking loudness is not the same as appreciating silence. It's not the lack of noise: *it's the space that houses all noise.* Silence is not just a lack of sound, it is what gives birth to sound. Music wouldn't be what it is if those sacred spaces of silence between the notes didn't exist. In silence, we create a space to realize the life-force that we are – the beating heart, our breath and an awareness. It's immensely powerful, and therefore extremely intimidating to most of us. We numb ourselves with television, the radio, Facebook, Twitter or just human chatter any moment there is a lull in the day.

We employ so many things to cover up the space between the activities of the day. We are scared, scared to experience silence, because we are inherently aware of its power. We are scared that it has the potential to teach us the deepest nuggets of life, but it's scary up there. Just spend 15 minutes in silence and you will know the mayhem it can cause. Of course, silence for most of us is accompanied by incessant thought. That's why meditation is kept at arm's length by so many people. It all comes rushing down ... Boom! Boom! Boom! The thoughts cause havoc. But that doesn't say as much about silence as it does about our thoughts. It's actually a completely revolutionary experience if we spend the 15 minutes actually *seeing* our thoughts. Silence gives us the space to do that exercise. Our inner world is spaciousness and silence – that is who we are. When we appreciate and seek it, it's nothing but a deep recognition of the silence that is inside all of us.

Someone wise once told me a story about a man who lost his key. He fiercely kept looking for his key in his garden in broad daylight. A passerby asked if he could help and joined in on the search for the lost key. After a while, the passerby asked the man where exactly he lost it. The man answered that he lost it inside the house. The flustered passerby asked why then were they searching outside. To that the man answered, "*Because it's dark inside*"!

Most of us are looking for our keys outside, even though the answers lie inside. The single biggest transformation in my life has been the discovery of silence and then the befriending of it.

Silence gives us the opportunity to feel our inner world. I love the magnificence of the simple but powerful exercise in Eckhart Tolle's *Power of Now*. He says, "Ask yourself, what I am feeling right now?" and then just hear. My personal experience is that my whole body feels alive, as if every cell in my body is saying, "I am present!" I believe with conviction that you can only appreciate the present moment when you have a deep appreciation and awareness of silence.

Takeaway

My urge to you is to invite silence to your life early. Try and sit in silence for five minutes every day. Just appreciate the tree in front of your balcony or the potted plant in your room. When you feel comfortable, increase the time. Because unless we can practice silence without getting terrorized by it, we will not be able to access the vast intelligence that is right behind the layer of thought chatter. You will soon realize that 24X7 guide that you always have at your disposal. I often find myself asking a question that's troubling me and then waiting in silence. Soon, I get an answer with uncanny clarity. Why wait to get introduced to something so powerful that can help us to live a magnificent life, why wait at all? It is the single most underrated tool out there in the market. Can you believe this therapist is free? You can access it right here, right now at no cost!

Moment of contemplation:

Observe your thoughts for five minutes.

Were you uncomfortable during that exercise? If so, what caused the discomfort?

____

____

____

____

"What do you really want?"

"What everyone wants. To be happy no matter what."

The Goal is Not Happiness

"Happiness is the absence of striving for happiness."

~Chuang Tzu

Dear P,

I see no reason why anyone, especially teens, should wait to start their spiritual journey. Absolutely none. I disagree that spiritual insights are far too deep for teens or they still have some 'growing up' to do. Because of the exhaustive list of external and internal changes teens go through, most of them are much deeper in their thoughts than is apparent (sometimes way too much!). Comprehension is high because it needs to be; otherwise the race is difficult to survive.

I know exactly what you're going through right now because I was there. You are going through the flow of everyday life with a blanket of gloom. There are days that bring you joy and there are ones that make you distraught. Life seems to oscillate between these two polarities by virtue of things happening in the world external to you. Things happen and you react, positively or otherwise. *It's like you are on a boat and you have no way to steer it. It's just going*. High waves throw water into the boat and storms deflect the boat in the direction of their choice. I get every ounce of the frustration you are feeling right now. The question I often asked myself was *"What are you looking for Priyanka?" "What is it?"* My answer was always "Happiness."

My parents grew up in modest homes where love was not a scarcity and they loved me dearly. I was loved and appreciated every day. I had the freedom to have hobbies and was encouraged to have a career of my choice. I ranked top three in my school and had a 4.0 GPA in grad school. I had wonderful jobs were I was appreciated and given amazing opportunities. I found love at the age of 15 and did not have to think about companionship for the rest of my life. My husband loves me beyond words. I travelled extensively to locations all around the world. I earned a six-figure salary before I turned 30 and lived on the 24th floor of a dreamy condo in Chicago with views of Lake Michigan and the most gorgeous sunsets.

I should have been happy.

But I was not. If I cannot be happy with the most favorable circumstances, can I ever be happy?

Most probably not.

Because I have realized that the happenings of our life can give us rippling feeling of happiness and unhappiness on the surface but fail to go any deeper. Nothing more. If I truly want to pursue happiness, it will be an endless pursuit. It's manic to do that.

After more than a decade of exploring the whims of happiness since my teens, I have come to land on something I have found peace with. *Happiness is dependent on external existential events that you and I have no control over.* The people, the places, the weather, all have to align for us to achieve the state of happiness. Happiness sits on a pedestal and we are in constant pursuit of it.

Eckhart Tolle says that there is a space between happiness and unhappiness – *Inner Peace.* That's where I found my answer. There are no polarities with inner peace and it's a very intimate phenomenon. It's ours and ours only to have. No one can mess with it, no one has ownership of our inner peace. I can be happy and be in peace and I can be supremely unhappy and still have my inner peace. It's the protective coating for the flame of our inner self.

Life is a constant stream of events, and the apparent intensity varies. If we are riled by life or the events in it, we have something to learn here. That is the beauty of life: it is designed to teach but we soften up to it only when we realize it is indeed working for us, not against. So, the first step is to give up resistance and accept that life has something to offer us in every situation. Events would not exist if they were not going to evolve us into something better. Also, events are impermanent. The resulting happiness and unhappiness are thus also impermanent. "This too will pass" is not a stretch of the imagination.

The goal is to reach a state of mental consistency, without the peaks or valleys of emotions that life often triggers. That's where our unflinching flame of inner peace lies. Otherwise we will live in fear of saying goodbye to the peaks, despise the time we are in the valley and live in the pursuit of peaks in the middle – we will just keep fighting, and that's no fun.

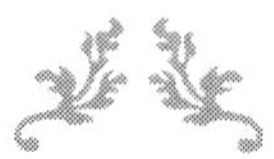

Takeaway

Whenever I find myself in a whirlwind, I create a picture which has become my haven. I imagine myself as a candle flame in the center of the whirlwind. Things, situations and strong feelings move around me but I stay still at the center. As I continue to focus on the flame, I realize that the whirlwind is completely separate than me and as long as I concentrate on the flame, the whirlwind cannot touch me. I keep that image in my vision for as long as it takes me to make believe that moment. Creating a vision of a safe place where I can rest during difficult moments has been hugely beneficial for me. My inner flame is my own. I guard my inner peace. Everything else comes and goes, it's just gravy.

Moment of contemplation:

Think of three things that come to mind about happiness.

Create three visions or pictures that have a soothing effect in your mind. Go back to these pictures whenever you feel turmoil building up.

"I have this nagging feeling that always fights the present."

"Why do you think you have this feeling?"

"I don't know. I just know it's always in the background, it barely goes away."

The Magic of Non-Resistance

"Acceptance of the unacceptable is the greatest source of grace in the world."

~Eckhart Tolle

Dear P,

I know that feeling of non-satisfaction growing in you. That sinking feeling that you don't want to be *here*. I wanted to be *there* when I had no idea of where 'there' is. I just knew that what *is* was not good for me. *I wanted something else.*

There is no end to things that can irk us in our time here on Earth this time around. Umpteen things can get us down, depress us, and spoil our day, week, year or worse, life. You didn't get into the college of your choice, or didn't get the coveted scholarship, the boy you like ignores you constantly, and you get passed over for promotion again. There is seriously no end to things you did not have or get. The interesting thing about this is that once you get sucked in, the story deepens, it becomes a downward spiral and you start believing that maybe, just maybe, your life is not meant to work. Period. Or my favorite: "I am just unlucky"!

I was no exception to this whirlwind. Situations, circumstances seem to hit me hard – pretty much all of them. I was vulnerable to any change from the status quo. A friend said something out of the ordinary, the teacher indicated she was not very happy with my assignment, my dad didn't look at me when he got back from work – it could be the neighborhood dog not wagging his tail hard enough and I was a ball of nerves. I soon realized that most circumstances of my life, other than the ones that were regular everyday events like brushing my teeth or taking a shower, were hitting me pretty hard. I resisted them with all of my heart. I just did not want to hear one harsh word, meet anyone who didn't adore me or anything that did not jive with my idea of a perfect day – which just meant that I was in a constant state of resistance to life.

I couldn't really relate the sinking dissatisfaction and my constant reaction of resistance to events in my life. I didn't realize that it was this resistance that was causing the dissatisfaction in my life.

I was torn after the realization, because acceptance is an incredibly hard fact to internalize. *"How can I accept someone even after they have called me names?" "My friend just met with an accident – how do I find acceptance there?"* I would find the peace of acceptance for some time and then I was back to fighting it.

I was looking for inspiration everywhere to make this journey easier and I stumbled upon something that resonated deeply. Nature. On looking deeper, I realized that nature never resists when the wind blows: the leaves sway with it. They let it be. Parts of the Earth live in darkness for hours every day. Earth never questions. When the rain falls, the sea level increases. It doesn't resist. It lets it be. The sky gives up its space to house the clouds. It goes with the flow and does nothing to drive them away. A perfectly nice garden can have weeds growing without any resistance from the flowers of the garden. It lets them be.

Then why do we resist the flow of life? Everything seems to be a fight, a struggle, like it is not meant to be. Maybe it's not meant to be and that's just OK. One of the many things that I took away from my journey from resistance to acceptance is to trust that the universe is on my side. It always is. But as much as it wants to do good for me, I have a part in this relationship too. I have to let it be. Just accept situations for what they are. Say YES to what's happening.

Sure, it feels bad, uneasy and uncomfortable for a while. But starting the practice of non-resistance early in life will ensure we don't spend our youth in varying expectations of the outside world and then fighting the resistance this accompanies. Non-resistance will bring the deep wisdom of knowing that we always have an ally in the universe, and the workings of the world are what they are. They are only capable of permeating into our ego and they are minuscule compared to the expanse of our inner world.

Reacting with non-resistance seems unnatural at first, but with practice, it will replace resistance as the natural reaction to untoward happenings in our life. Acceptance helps us conserve the energy we need to deal with these situations or people. Otherwise, the drama that ensues will sap us of this much-needed energy. Since the drama will usually take a downward spiral, it will exhaust us.

I lost my dear grandfather a few years ago. All through my adolescence and adulthood, I was terrified of losing him and facing the inevitable as he aged. I couldn't imagine a world where I couldn't hear his voice anymore. I remember the night when I got the news, I faced a shift. I accepted the situation, although my heart was broken. Suddenly, peace pervaded me as I lay down on my bed. I knew he was at peace. And so was I.

Acceptance creates space to think of a solution and for a higher self to speak directly to us. And in many cases, as in the death of a loved one, there is no solution. The space created by accepting the situation will allow us to grieve in a peaceful place of knowing.

Takeaway

Next time you are in a situation where you are tempted to fight and blow up – you missed a flight, you are stuck in a traffic jam or umpteen such situations – whisper to yourself, "I accept this." Repeat it a few more times until you align with the *suchness* of the event. Notice the peace coming to you. More often than not, the universe will reward you in some inexplicable fashion for embracing life with the grace of acceptance.

Moment of contemplation:

Describe a situation of great conflict in your life currently.

What are you resisting in this conflict?

____

____

____

____

"I didn't fare up to my expectations, yet again.
When will I be happy with my performance?"

"Have you ever been?"

"No."

Presence over Perfection

"The thing that is really hard, and really amazing, is giving up on being perfect and beginning the work of becoming yourself."

~Anna Quindlen

Dear P,

The best – that's what I wanted for most of my life. Anything less was unacceptable. I would take up a sport, a hobby, a subject matter, it didn't really matter what it was – my focus was always to fare better than anyone else. That was the goal. Period. That seemed like a great way to live – I was validated by friends and family time and again. It felt good to be the best.

The desire to be the best sits deep as we dive into the real-world pool. School, college and friends drive us to participate in the race and the finish line becomes our goal. Reach for the moon; shoot for the stars– we all grew up with these adages. Participation is appreciated, but competition is venerated beyond reason. There is a subliminal thirst to have that perfect finish, which in terms of this world is to finish *numero uno.* I was good at most things I took up – swimming, academics, athletics, or painting. But if you were to ask me the one thing that ruined all of these experiences for me, it was the feeling that my world would fall apart if I was not the best.

I fell in love with swimming. I would dive in and forget the world. I was a mermaid lost in my sea world. Then my coaches recognized that I had a gift. Training and advice grilled me every day. I could not be a mermaid anymore: I was a swimmer competing to be the best. Every mistake was corrected and a day when I couldn't beat everyone else in trials was supposed to be a bad day for me. And then it became something different. It became work. I was not in love with swimming anymore.

Another great love of mine was to express my thoughts in visuals.

I used to paint, sketch and draw for myself. It was a personal form of expression. I was not gifted in a traditional sense, but there was an authenticity in my visuals that spoke to whoever saw them. I had no formal training: it was me, my thoughts and my fingers. One fine morning when I was about 11, my mother told me there was a local painting competition and I could draw anything my heart desired. I agreed to go. It did not matter to me that anyone was there, it mattered that they gave me a piece of paper and some crayons. Later in the day, much to my parents' disbelief, I was given the first prize in the competition. I didn't think much of it, but my folks must have realized that they had ignored this 'gift' for far too long. Soon, I had a teacher and all kinds of fancy tools and resources to paint. I was also asked to create a schedule for when I would "practice art". Up until then, the only schedule I knew of was my heart knocking on my door saying that it was time to sit down and put those words into something visual. But now there were too many cooks in the kitchen, and my heart stopped knocking. That was the end of it.

As adolescents and teens, our love for anything springs from a very pure space. But the moment we expose the love to the world, the attention of society triggers an adulteration. I don't know where love for something stops and fear and ego take over. But I am sure there is a handoff. We are too vulnerable in our adolescence to resist. Competition is a form of fear and the world we live in constantly tries to put a positive spin on it. We live at different levels of fear of abandonment if we cannot emerge as the winner of the race.

The problem is not that competition is bad; instead it is the fact that when we reach for the stars, we have our eyes set on nothing else. We are oblivious to everything beautiful that passes by. We miss out on the journey. And there festers a deep disappointment when we settle for something less because we were so attached to the outcome. Soon we find ourselves in a really dark place accompanied by a deep sense of lack.

The number one spot comes with its own anti-climax. When we do achieve the spot, there is a quick high, a fleeting moment of grandeur, and then it all fades. The 'best' is transient, because soon someone else takes our place and we set a higher milestone for ourselves. There is now a new star in the sky! A new benchmark of perfection ensues and we stay on the treadmill for a really long time.

There are a zillion things I missed out on because just participating and enjoying my participation was not good enough for me. I look back and think about the play I could have done, the choir I could have joined, the sports team that could have used my incredible agility and determination in, or how I could have continued my passion for swimming. But I was fearful of not being the best. That's why I didn't do them.

What I have realized after crashing and burning many times over the pursuit of being the best was that it is a fallacy of the mind. It's the ego that's trying to become whole by one more story – the story of me being the best, and then not anymore, then again and not anymore. Both outcomes are equally entertaining to the ego. When perfection is the goal, fear abstains fun from showing up in the journey. Adolescence is about experiences; in fact the whole of life is a string of experiences. At the end of it, it doesn't really matter how we fared: it matters we went through it.

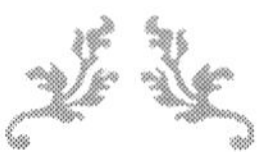

Takeaway

Be in the moment and enjoy what you are doing. When you happen to land on great success, know that it was the result of letting a higher intelligence, your deeper self, work through you. That higher- self shows up when we are having fun or lost in an activity because we love it so much. Success, when it's an outcome of enjoying the journey is a different win – it's the winning of the self over the stories of the mind. Don't let your success be just another story that your mind can play with. It's just another moment. Enjoy it and then let it go. Make space for the next ...

Moment of contemplation:

What are the areas in your life where you feel fiercely competitive?

What do you fear you will lose if you are not the very best in those fields?

___

___

___

___

"You have a gift, I know that. You know that."

"I am scared it will reveal itself."

Honoring Our Sacred Gifts

"We are each gifted in a unique and important way. It is our privilege and our adventure to discover our own special light."

~Mary Dunbar

Dear P,

Our gifts are sacred. They are also hugely undermined by their carriers. When I first took to writing, it was a little *Mansfield Park* journal that no one was allowed to touch. The reason being it was sacred, which I still hold to be true, but the other reason confused me for a long time. *I didn't want other people to make fun of me.* The consideration that anyone could find what I write to be good enough seemed far-fetched.

My writing gave me great solace in times of darkness. I would read and re-read my essays, notes and poems and come out feeling energized. But it was not for the world. We can call that a lot of things – lack of self-esteem or self-confidence. But it was something more...

- I didn't consider writing to be my gift
- A part of me knew that writing was absolutely my gift
- I was not ready to change my life due to my gift
- I was not ready for my family and friends to perceive me differently
- I realized eerily how powerful my gift *could* be

With deep trepidation, I submitted my first essay on an online site. A lot of things went through my mind – will my friends see me through a different lens? Will my family think that I am crazier than they thought I was? What will my husband think of me? This is not 'normal.' Do I really need this? Should I send them a note to ignore my post? I came very close to, "*Sorry, I sent this by mistake*," but something stopped me. Part of me was ready to face the fear. Then came the comments, and with them some much-needed clarity. A lady wrote to me that the post was "*just what she needed to read at that time.*" Another comment noted that the words "really resonated" with them. In that moment, I knew why I wrote. Why I wrote anything at all. It didn't have to be any bigger. She got me. He got me. This was not redemption. This was realization.

I started looking around and studying my friends – each one had a gift I could uniquely recognize. Some could sketch beautifully, some could write computer code like a breeze, some were awesome facilitators and then there were the soulful artists. While some got out, many of them are still journaling in their own way, just like I did.

What is a gift, after all? We can call it our gift, our purpose, our personal legend or the calling – they all point to the same thing. It is the constant knock on the door. It is that underlying feeling that there is something more and that there is a dire need to address it. The urgency of it is directly proportional to our act of ignoring our gifts. This urgency manifests itself in many innovative ways – I have personally experienced it as restlessness, unprecedented boredom, lack of aliveness and a general feeling that life is passing me by, coupled with bouts of sessions when I would cry without reason. But the most destructive manifestation was in addictions, I was addicted to sweets and I would eat with a vengeance. It took me awhile to get to the bottom of that one. We often tend to turn to compulsions and addictions to drown out that urgent voice. We keep trying until we reach a breaking point and finally pay heed.

We are scared! We are scared to recognize our gifts because then we are obligated to do something about it. As long as it sits in the journal, in the basement, in the closet, in our minds – we can carry on with our normal lives. The moment we acknowledge it, we have to honor it.

But we are also deeply aware, although we may not accept that our gifts when brought to the world can have a profound impact even if we live completely unaware of it. We are cultured to think that this might be a case of self-glorification or narcissism. *How could we have any impact on other people? How preposterous of us!* Our social thinking overrides our belief in our gifts.

Then there is the case of 'no one will get us.' It is always too abstract, too deep, very crazy or extremely out there. It makes us uncomfortable to think that no one will buy our work. It will just rot, out in the world.

There are several such stories that we tell ourselves. Fear cripples us. The good news is, since we created them, we have the power to demolish them. Our gifts are not of the material world. They germinate at the spirit level and our recognition of their pure energy causes a resonance with the universe. Once we decide to listen to that constant humming and listen carefully, we start connecting with the formless. There is no fear and there is no expectation at that level.

I don't think that it is our job to worry about what happens to our work after it is out in the world. Our contract is to honor that hidden pot of joy that we constantly resist but secretly revere, to give it the nurturing it requires to be, not perfect, but just the best version that it could be at that point in our lives. What happens to it after is up to the universe.

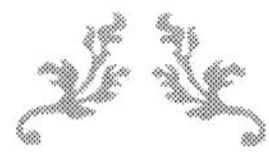

Takeaway

Someone somewhere is going to get it. We really need only one to make it worthwhile, if at all that needs to be proven. I am not setting expectations low, but our gifts do not necessarily have to be on the bestseller list. They just need to *be received.* If the fear of not being on the list discourages us from getting our work out there, imagine that person whose life we could have impacted right when they needed it, but didn't. So publish that book, send the painting to the gallery, start that blog, open that business, put up that homemade jewelry online, frame those sketches and make that record – someone, somewhere has been waiting for it ...

Moment of contemplation:

What are your sacred gift(s)?

What steps do you take daily or weekly to honor them?

State your fears, if any, around getting them out in the world.

"Why do you crave attention?"

"If people don't notice, what's the point anyway?"

Please Approve of Me!

"The only approval, the only validation and the only opinion that matters in the quest for our greatness is our own."

~Steve Maraboli

Dear P,

There are so many addictions that we focus on in our society. Smoking, drinking, drugs, you name it. Very rarely do we talk about the omnipresent addiction – our need for someone's approval. This addiction has cost the human race big time. It has killed many dreams, destroyed umpteen relationships, kept millions of creative work of all sorts from coming out into the world.

It is also very sneaky. It enters from the background and relentlessly urges us to seek approval. *"Will people approve of me if I move into this house, buy this car, and get this job title or the very interesting one, when I join this non-profit"?* Even in the most honest intentions, this need for approval sneaks in and begs for attention.

Growing up, I felt the need to bring pride, joy and happiness into my parents' lives. For everything that they had done for me, I felt the need to inundate them with small and big joys. When I won competitions, I came back home and looked them in the eye for the glimmer of approval. Every time I brought a medal home and called out to my dad, "Dad, see what I got," Dad beamed and his eyes moistened. There was a certain rush within me when I saw that. The eyes that approve are the most beautiful eyes! Aren't they? Somewhere in this process, I developed a deep-seated habit of seeking that rush again and again. It's like I had tasted the drug and now I wanted to go get some more.

I have made many bad decisions because of this unrelenting need to be approved. Denial of this truth plagued me for a very long time. On the outside, I portrayed that I didn't really care for anyone. Why do I need others? I was enough. The truth was that I wasn't enough. Or I didn't know I was. I could only realize myself when someone said something nice about me, or liked what I was doing. I needed to fill myself up with praise and appreciation. I couldn't deny it any longer.

The thing about this addiction are the highs and lows. The highs felt quite good, but the lows, oh man, those really brought me down. I didn't take so many risks because I didn't want to feel the lows. I hated myself during them, as part of me recognized how rigged the game is and felt sorry about the potential I knew I was putting at risk.

The one thing that turned this around for me was realizing that there is no one else but me who can satiate my need in a meaningful way. And that empty bottle that was seeking love and acknowledgment – it's looking for me to do it. I get to fill the bottle with love, connection and respect for myself. In addition, I curbed the impact by recognizing and questioning when the feeling to seek approval crept in and trying to catch it before it got to spread its wings. Connecting with myself via meditation helped strengthen my relationship with myself. Spending time in silence where I could confront this deeply personal and uncomfortable behavior pattern really helped to release it from my space.

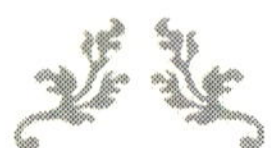

Takeaway

If you feel that there is a pattern developing within you to seek approval from the outside, the first step of recognition is complete. Great! Now starts the job of positive feedback to yourself so that you can respectfully let the pattern go, without putting up a fight.

- Forgive yourself for seeking approval. It's called being human.
- This pattern is indicative of a calling to seek an alignment of your body, mind and spirit.
- Acknowledge your own joys and focus on them.
- Question decisions that are based on external approval. Take time out. Don't give this pattern any airtime during important moments in your life.

We are hardwired to respond to and seek external approval. We just have to reverse the wiring by building the right muscles. As we build the muscles to tackle this pattern, the responses will become quicker and require increasingly less effort.

Moment of contemplation:

Can you recognize in yourself the need to seek approval?

Can you trace this pattern back to events in the past? What were they?

"No matter what I do, I can't fight this feeling of dread."

"Then don't fight it."

"But something within doesn't want to give in."

Gift of Surrender

"Surrender becomes so much easier when you realize the fleeting nature of all experiences and that the world cannot give you anything of lasting value."

~Eckhart Tolle

Dear P,

One thing you can be completely sure of in life is to be challenged, to various degrees. There will be plenty of times when you will feel that life is not turning out well. There are many society-created success criteria and charters of how life ought to be. Your peers will constantly strive for this man-made dictum and, barring exceptions, your elders will say no different. Needless to say, the plague will catch onto you as well, and you will spend the rest of your living moments upholding societal dogmas and expectations.

There will be days when you will cry your heart out because you tried your best and failed, words didn't come out of your mouth in a debate competition, you didn't pass an important exam, didn't get the coveted job right out of – these societal milestones bog us down and we will indeed find some people laughing at us. You bet they will. Because ridiculing someone else puts them on a higher pedestal and bestows on them the high of a pseudo win. Later in your life, you will find yourself at several crossroads – choosing a major, picking a job, to study further or work, this guy or that, love over family honor, not clearing qualifying exams after the nth attempt. You will feel alone and tired. So tired.

After years of lamenting over challenges in life, I have finally found the panacea that heals in the darkest moments: Surrender. It's really as simple as that. *Let go of the reins that you never really had in the first place.*

As I look back at my life, every challenge has been caused by an inner fight between what I wanted from my life and the flow of life. "*This is not right," "This is not what I want," "Life is always tough on me," "I don't like this assignment," "I know I will fail again," "That's how my life is," "My flight is canceled again," "This sucks!"* I didn't want to flow with life: there were destinations that I thought that we had to reach that life never promised me. My mind showed me a glimpse of a flag post based on social expectations and made me believe that it was best for me. I never considered whether it wasn't. What if life has something else in store for me that will all make sense in the long run? Every time I followed a flag post aimlessly, I felt misaligned and a sense of great hollowness. I felt farther away from my purpose, even if I didn't know what my purpose was. I got into a habit of saying "no" to everything that arose in my life in the present, because the future always looked better ... in my mind. I always had better grades, friends, social situation, popularity, job, and appearance … in the future. Why enjoy anything that's right now because the future looks so much better than what I have right now?

But here is the biggest trick life has played on us. There is no future. It only exists in our mind. I realized that the biggest reason behind my dullness, boredom and overall apathy toward life was because I was running away from right 'here' to right 'there' and 'there' did not even exist.

Our realistic, pragmatic minds cannot fathom the workings of the formless world. We don't believe in anything we cannot see. But sometimes, we just have to learn to let go, let go of trying to make sense, of applying logic, much like we do about the miraculous process of conceiving to the actual birth of a baby. It is unreal if you really think about the intricacies of human anatomy working together to nurture a fetus, but humanity has surrendered to it and we don't think about it logically. We know it will take care of itself. We don't have to worry about feeding the baby in the womb or keeping it warm. We have surrendered that 'something' has it covered and it will be just fine!

Then why can't we believe that 'something' will take care of us when we ask for it? That we can forever dodge life's curveballs and that the universe is our BFF and will guide us to what's best?

Oprah Winfrey's story on surrender is my favorite. She wanted to be part of the movie based on Alice Walker's classic work *The Color Purple*. After a passionate audition, she didn't hear back and on trying to follow up was given a very discouraging answer. In despair, she found herself surrendering to a higher power. She asked God to help her let go of the hurt and bitterness if she didn't get the part. In a mystical moment, she found herself singing "I surrender all" and felt a weight had been lifted off her. Soon after, she was informed that she had got the iconic part of Sofia in the movie.

Surrender doesn't always lead to a positive outcome, but it makes us neutral to the outcome which in the end is anything but negative. Life is what's happening in this moment. Both the past and future are not real and conceptual at their best. When we surrender to the 'what is,' it's a shout-out to the world that we believe and trust in everything it has to offer.

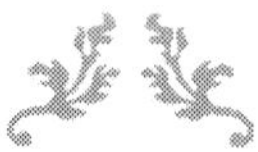

Takeaway

Every time a conflict appears, recognize and let go of the resistance to it. What has come to surface right at that moment is what life is. Life is Now. Everything else is resistance to Now. If we cannot be with life, we will be in resistance. And that's painful as well as futile. Things that have worked for me:

- If I find myself in an unwanted situation which I cannot walk out of, I say a quick prayer to myself: "I surrender to what's happening right now, knowing it's for my best interest. It will all make sense at the end."

- I plan my week ahead so my appointments and projects are not competing for my time. Once that is done, I focus only on the project at hand and avoid wondering if I should be somewhere else.

- I don't expect life to make me happy every moment. Life never promised such a thing.

Moment of contemplation:

Is there a situation in your life currently that you completely dislike? What are you resisting?

If you mentally allow the situation to be the way it is, do you experience anything different?

"I didn't want to lie today, but I did."

"Why?"

"I just thought it would make things easier ..."

No Shame in Truth

"Three things cannot be long hidden – the sun, the moon and the truth."

~Buddha

Dear P,

Fear pushes us to the fringes and compels us to do a lot of unwanted things – one of them is engaging in dishonesty. If you are plagued by fear in your life, chances are you will lie, even pretty often. Teens develop a lot of insecurities. I did. I did not want to displease anyone. If anything, I wanted to turn it around for them – even if that meant that I had to lie. How does it even matter? I thought – one tiny lie has not hurt anyone. Now these are not malicious lies, only the types we called white lies, which seem silly to the point of "why would you even say it?" There was a time when I compulsively lied – speaking the truth almost seemed like a lie in itself.

It was just another instance where my ego completely bullied me – another instance where I was not in touch with myself. If only I knew the hurt I was causing others – and myself. I knew I had to dig into the root, because otherwise the symptoms would keep reappearing. After all, why was I making things up? Why didn't I honor the facts?

After introspecting long and hard, I found that the core reason for me to do this was the fear of making someone unhappy, losing friends, not being everyone's favorite and just not being in their best books. So, I would try to change reality to make friends and family happy. It seemed like the perfect solution to create a sense of stability. Boy, was I wrong! As always with lying, it caught up with me. Embarrassment aside, it was the hurt that I had caused people closest to me that was devastating. In some cases, the things I said were so trivial, my jaw dropped at my own stupidity.

With the new realization, now it was up to me to make amends, to change my selection process and always choose truth, no matter how hard the internal resistance was. After all, it was years of programming that I had to undo.

It was my husband who taught me the value of truth above all else. He taught me to say what it is in every situation, no matter the magnitude of the inner resistance I faced. There should be no alternative to truth. There is none. We have no right to distort reality to make someone feel at ease. And in most cases, the truth never killed anyone. If I can't go to someone's party and tell them just that, I wouldn't lose them as a friend. As with a lot of things, I made the consequences up in my head. It turned out that I was lying to myself first and then distributing the message to other people.

Life is simple if we come from a place of love and truth. There are plenty of ways to attract drama into our lives – lying is one of them. If we speak the truth, we are always right, no matter how wrong we make someone or ourselves feel. We are always right in the arms of truth. Because embracing truth is embracing the present moment.

Takeaway

Embrace honesty in life – this time and every time. As I experienced, in lieu of some temporary pain, I received a much simpler life and cutting out the unnecessary complexity that lies always bring along. We can all do without that upkeep. We already have enough on our plate!

Moment of contemplation:

Do you feel you are being pressured to say a lie to please someone?

What or who is the source of this pressure?

What would you lose if you spoke the truth?

"You know, there are these very fleeting moments when I think about who I really am?"

"What happens next?"

"The moment ends before I can do anything with it."

Asking the First Big Question

"The thought 'Who Am I' will destroy all other thoughts, and like the stick used for stirring the burning pyre, it will itself in the end get destroyed. Then there will arise Self- Realization."

~Ramana Maharshi

Dear P,

Teenage brings along more than a few twisters – some small, some big. Needless to say, we often feel torn apart. Between these moments of great despair, sometimes, a door opens for fleeting moments of time that call for us to explore. I call this the "Who Am I" door. For a second, there seems to be a gap between our life and us. We may not have the words to articulate it, but something in us feels it in our gut. We may not talk about it with our friends or family: how do we? There are no words to define these experiences. But they are real.

Who am I?...arriving at the question itself is an adventure. It's not a frivolous question; I find this question to be the convergence point of all of life's experiences that we have had so far. The fact that we have dis-identified with our body for a moment and can even imagine that there can be something beyond is miraculous and awesome news for this planet.

A few years back, I was Priyanka Chatterjee – an Indian, a Bengali, an immigrant in the US, working in a certain profession...I had some descriptive and a set of defining attributes. I liked this, I didn't like that. I liked these people, that set was just not my type. That was my story. The story of who I am. But it's only when I stepped out of my story for a second that I could consider that my story and me may be separate. Is there a possibility that who I really am is not a story but something that's more consistent and universal?

I am going to cut to the chase: *my chase*. You might grow up to find a different interpretation of life and who you really are. And you should. It's almost like we live our whole life and go through the set of experiences in order to finally arrive at an answer to this big question. But this is where I am arriving at after the last few years of exploration, knowing well that my answers will keep evolving or deepening.

Who I really am is an ageless, non-destructive, non-intimidated, un-attached, peaceful, calm and formless being who has found an abode in this benevolent body. Everything else is a story. I am indeed consistent with the whole of mankind. We are all *That*. Our stories are very different. We are different in the superficial, we are not different at the core.

With this comes the understanding that everyone – our closest circle of friends, the family members who we may not particularly like, the friends who are perpetually mean, are all *That*. They are all the same I. Where we differ is in the physical and our conditioned thought patterns, which matters in this material world but not really in the bigger picture.

But what does this knowledge do to us? How does this change anything?

This drives me to try to not carry over grudges, be too sensitive to hurtful comments and to forgive easily – because I know these are caused by the drama of life and the participants of this drama are all really the same entity, wearing different masks. That's why I find politics, fascism, intolerance toward diversity and religious battles to be extremely nonsensical. We are all fighting mind-based fictitious entities, completely forgetting that we are fighting oneness, we are fighting against each other to save each other, since we are all really one spirit. If this is not a dysfunction, what is?

Takeaway

Take some time out and ask the question "Who am I?" and listen for the answer. Feel the answer, don't analyze. Come back to this often. And in the midst of despair in human relationships, consider for a second that all of us are the same in the core. We differ at the shell level. Now view your dynamics with these new pair of eyes.

Moment of contemplation:

Close your eyes and ask the question "Who am I"? For every answer you get, ask the question "Who is it that's asking, thinking or answering this?" Write down some of the responses here.

II. WHILE IN THE WORLD

"Sometimes I feel like I am in a movie or a story."

"Why?"

"It just feels prewritten or that I am living out a blueprint."

You Are Here to Experience It All

"Wealth is the ability to fully experience life."

~Henry David Thoreau

Dear P,

"Why am I here" is a very important question in our life journey. You might have never asked this question literally yet, but it's all building up to it. One day you will feel it, even if you don't ask. Sometimes the question just lingers in us, waiting for the right time. The asking of this question, I believe, is the beginning of the shift in consciousness in us. And therefore, I rejoice when someone asks or discusses this question, publicly or in a candid conversation. It is also an indication that the world is rising above the material realm and we are ready to open the door to a new consciousness.

We are here to experience it all – the good, the bad, and the ugly. The human experience must be a fascinating journey for the spirits, something they undertake knowing all the risks. Of course, the rigmarole of life is so engaging that the souls completely identify with the human experience, forgetting where they started out. But that's a different note altogether!

We are here to take it all in – birth, learning how to walk, learning the good and the bad, making choices, playing out our jobs, falling in love, breaking our heart, losing a loved one, feeling attachment to things, losing the things we are attached to, having a child, teaching our children to walk, getting old, seeing glimpses of approaching death – everything!

I look at life as being given the entry into a humongous amusement park. There are millions of rides – small and big, just like the different experiences of our lives. The rides are of different risk levels and you choose the risk level on entry. The risk levels lead you into different sections of the park, and therefore everyone gets separated even though they started at the same point. You meet other people in the park as well, who have received the same entry pass as you. Some take the rides, while some are full of fear and prefer sitting at the sidelines. Some like the ambitious and exciting rides that trigger their adrenaline, others take it slow. Some bliss out on their rides, while some have really bad experiences. But somewhere down the line, most of us get so consumed by the rides and the experiences that we forget that we are in an amusement park after all – by the heat or the intense crowd or the fact that your favorite rides have a mechanical failure. We lose the amusement. We forget why we were there at the first place. Then, at the end of the day, when it's time to leave, we feel so spent and wonder if we just wasted our time and that if given a chance could we have played it differently.

In my experience, the only reason we live is to give our spirit a physical form to be able to experience life. We chose to come into this life, our very life with the vagaries it presents. If we didn't have a body, we wouldn't feel the breeze on our face, our hair blowing in the wind, the passion of a lover, the smell of a beautiful rose. We would be in another dimension, living it up, you know. But we wouldn't be able to experience anything first-hand. We would have to depend on stories we heard or whatever mechanics spirits use in that realm.

Yes, there are soul contracts and karmic reasons for our presence on this planet. We are here to close out our ties and experience the divine emotions of love, compassion and service. Yes, there are spiritual laws in place for why we incarnate, but above all what life boils down to for me is the myriad of experiences and our learning from them. It's important that we are conscious of these experiences – it's paramount that we don't go through life in a stupor, taking each day for granted. Otherwise, lifetime after lifetime we go through the rigmarole of similar situations because the experience is waiting for us to acknowledge it with our presence.

Takeaway

For me, we are here to experience it all, consciously. Every experience has layers of meaning, and our consciousness will bring these forth without us trying at all. So experience every moment in awe. And keep amusement handy, please.

Moment of contemplation:

List some of your top life experiences.

Contemplate what would happen if you did not have a human form in the context of these experiences, e.g. *I would not feel the exhilaration of riding a roller coaster.*

"What brings you joy? True joy."

"Hmm, I don't know. Watching the fluttering of the tree leaves, maybe."

Recognizing Our *Joytivities*

"My general formula for my students is 'Follow your bliss.' Find where it is, and don't be afraid to follow it."

~Joseph Campbell

Dear P,

Most of my early adulthood has gone into discovering what I want to 'do' in my life. Quotes like "*Find out what you want to do,*" "*What do you love to do?,*" "*Find your calling through your work*" did nothing to help the uproar inside. It only made it worse. Destiny, calling, etc. just seemed like buzz words that were not credible.

The growing awareness that one might be here to do something very specific can be utterly frustrating, because it comes without a map or directions. But this awareness is special. In many ways, the source of this frustration maybe the germination of your spiritual journey, as it was for me. A by-product of this phenomenon is restlessness and restlessness so severe that it would bring me to my knees. This very feeling pushed me to dabble in multiple jobs, activities and social relationships. I was keenly aware when something didn't align. There was an eerie discomfort, a sense of not being at the right place and my favorite – trying way too hard to like something. When any of these three conditions were met, I knew it was time to move on.

I loved reading as a child. Devouring books not only gave me a sense of joy, I lost all track of time or meals. The mind cleared out and it was the book, me and a sense of calm in between. When I reluctantly kept the book aside, I felt my soul get a boost and something soared from the inside. It almost sat back up, spine straight and said "now, I am ready for some trigonometry!" Stated simply, I felt good. Reading was my haven when anything in the world went wrong. It rejuvenated my soul. However, I never thought much of writing. I have been journaling from my preteens and never really acknowledged that I went back to writing when I needed some peace. Writing genuinely made me happy. One day, a friend casually asked me, "*What is the one thing you do when there is no one at home and you are all by yourself, something that you completely lose yourself in*"? I didn't even think twice … it was always writing. Whether it was journaling, writing poems or essays – nothing gave me as much peace and a sense of alignment than putting pen to paper.

Years later, when I started working in technology consulting, I found myself really enjoying the aspect of working with clients and helping people gain a new perspective about the business. In addition, coaching or training new employees became an activity that gave me immense joy.

Over the years, I started to understand and recognize my joys more consciously. Tracking my joys has helped me land on an important perspective: we don't need to find the perfect job, activity or hobby; we just have to find our *joytivities* ... activities that fill us with great joy. The recognition of things that bring us joy is a huge step in our evolution, no matter how small they are.

Smelling the soil after rain, enjoying the magnificence of a sunrise, the nostalgia of a sunset, the roar of the ocean, walking through nature, reading, writing, listening to someone talk, learning about a particular subject, getting a tattoo, bungee jumping, being around animals, sitting on the couch with your favorite candle lit or what have you ... we need to acknowledge the things we like to do that bring us immense joy. They are the guiding flag posts of our own version of a happy life. Our ideal external job in this lifetime, if we can overcome the guilty pleasures of money, power and prestige, will be a combination of the things that we most enjoy doing. Most people ignore this and might still be very successful in their jobs. But if they ever made an honest confession about their professional lives, they would talk about the constant restlessness and a deep-seated void. And while our sorrows and daily life drama hog the limelight and consume our lives, our joys are always there for our taking and need no tending. We just need to reach out.

Takeaway

Activities that are therapeutic for us also give us a glimpse of who we really are – we see a very pure form of us when we are engaged in our *joytivities*. It is not important for them to become our job. As long as we are able to disengage ourselves from the rigmarole of our daily lives and spend as much time as we can engaging in these activities, there is a shift within us. Interestingly, devoting time to our joys helps us to experience serenity and calm in all other areas of our lives – such is the power of connecting to our joys. It is a meditation indeed.

Moment of contemplation:

Think about three activities that bring you immense joy. Indicate how each of these activities makes you feel.

____

____

____

____

"I can't. I just can't decide on my career – what to do, where to go. I just feel lost."

"What is the end goal for you?"

"Money? Success? More money?"

Figuring Out That Career

"Your career is your business. It's time for you to manage it as a CEO."

~Anonymous

Dear P,

Indecision, frustration, worry, anxiety, adventure – every emotion you are feeling about deciding your career has been felt by others. The road to arriving at a career can be a potpourri, but people have traveled the road before. They may have bruises, but each one symbolizes a shift that makes life meaningful. Unless we are couch potatoes, any reasonable person striving for a dream or an aspiration feels the pangs of rejection and fear. We are better off for it. For every struggle we boldly face, there is one more ethic we build that is going to serve us for the rest of our lives. Don't be resistant to this phase; embrace it with all your heart, because it's here to change you for the better. Through the journey of my own career soul-searching, here are some key learnings I came across in my path:

It's OK to not know what you are good at. It feels uncomfortable, I know. But it's really OK. We cross a certain age and people start asking a seemingly profound question – "*What do you think you will do with your career? What are you good at?*" At 15, I was good at reading, dancing all goofy and staring at trees. Now, I would be called a 'case' if I mentioned that these activities were my interests. What I am trying to say is that life is a journey to find ourselves. If we knew exactly who we are and what we would like to do as a career, we wouldn't need to go through life. Choosing a career path is important, but the trial and error approach comes in very handy if you are like me. Be OK to try out something and then not like it. You may find yourself being compared to that peer who made it big in a job and is now making the big bucks – but life has a way of leveling itself out – just trust that process and keep on keeping on.

Define success for yourself. What does success mean to you? Not the societal definitions but your own. The quick responses at this age are usually money, a fancy car, a fun relationship, great parties, etc. Challenge yourself as to whether indeed this is your idea of success. Some people find success in stable relationships, some in great ambition – everyone needs to define it for themselves, beyond the apparent. The earlier you do this, the easier it will be to make choices. So, when your boss asks you to come out for a drink on your mom's birthday, you will know the best decision intuitively.

Determine your bliss. Even as you go through the decision-making process to determine a career, be completely certain of what you really like to do. And it does not have to be grandiose. It can be as simple as "I like to talk to people," "I like to help people in need," or, "I like to listen to people when they want to talk." Understanding what gives us joy helps maneuver us in a way that can lead to a life which involves those things. Often we get into a profession because of peer pressure or a desire for quick money, and soon enough that profession becomes our routine. If you don't find bliss in what you do day in and day out, life can become morose and unsatisfying.

Money is not the end goal. There is no denying that money is important. It provides us with the necessary validations in material and nonmaterial forms. But here is the twist to this story. The moment survival is in the bag – you get the apartment, the TV, the car – you question the overall purpose of life. Even if this does not happen directly, inner restlessness will implore you go deeper than the apparent needs and wants. As you take the next steps, realize that money is important to meet the basic human needs, but there is a tipping point where money ceases to provide you with the answers you seek internally. Be prepared to not feel completely satisfied with a bank balance. And be open to exploring the restlessness when it arrives.

Never ignore well-being. Working hard is good. We are trained in our ethos to work the hardest we can. But here is the thing: nothing is more important than our health and well-being. There are a lot of people who work really hard and are successful but are burdened by depression, diabetes, heart disease and cannot walk more than 300ft. That's neither success nor how life deserves to be treated. As you walk into your career, remember to take good care of your health. At the end of the road, our health determines our quality of life, irrespective of the assets or job titles we possess.

Make every day count. A stable career means an average of 10-hour days starting every morning – take a shower, get ready, grab breakfast (if at all), work the next 8 hours on marketing campaign/strategy document/ make presentations/ make deals/negotiations (or whatever the heck we do), come (mostly to an empty) home, fix dinner, sleep – now do it all over again the next day. When we finally settle down into a career, which we strive for so hard, it's about making every day count – even though it's the same thing every day. To that extent, it doesn't matter what we do at all. How we live every day is exponentially more important to focus on – were you kind to your colleagues today? Were you patient with your clients? Did you show integrity in your work? Did you strive to get better at something? It's in the 'being,' not necessarily always in the 'doing.'

Love. It's a cliché but it really is the only thing that matters. If you are devoid of love in your life – love of a partner, love of family, and love of friends – your career can only fill the void temporarily. People do crazy things to fill that void – buy things, get angry, buy more things. It doesn't help. A lot of addictions can find their foundations in a deep desire to love and be loved. Prioritize relationships and family over temporary pleasures early so that you keep reaping the benefit through most of your life. At the very end, very few people think of the hours spent in their cubicles. It's always the moments and memories made with people that truly matter.

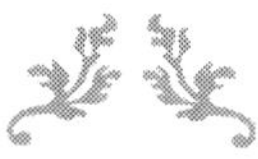

Takeaway

Clarity about our own self is subtly the most important thing when choosing a career. Our careers will be a medium of self-discovery. As hard as it gets, try and enjoy the ride. It's not as serious as you are taking it. As long as we can treat our careers as an extension of our authentic self, we will be at peace, which as you will realize soon enough is so much more important than "success".

Moment of contemplation:

What are three things that you seek in your career?

Do you have principles that your career should make room for? What are they? How flexible are you with them? Or are they non-negotiable?

"I feel restless through the day. I feel anxious like there is an impending doom coming."

"Why do you think that is?"

"I don't know."

Selective Absorption

"The soul does not absorb negativity by accident, only by choice."

~Dodinsky

Dear P,

I remember soaking up the morning newspaper to get out of the morning daze right after waking up. I took in all the world and the media had to tell me – the good, the bad and the very ugly – which plane crashed, who was murdered and the minute by minute update on genocides across the world. And I realized how my mind was wired to receive bad to really bad news – I thought it was all very normal!

Turning on CNN first thing in the morning became a habit. Incessant bashing up of the newly elected president continued 24/7 and I really enjoyed it. I grew concerned when watching positive programs made me crave some negativity, some drama. I was addicted to negative news.

Growing up offered a lot of sources of information from news channels, innocent gossip that seemed to be ever-prevailing and then the bombardment of materials like the presidential debates that rile a nation like no other trigger. The more I indulged, the more drained I felt. The content is negative but surprisingly enticing. The stimulating power of these materials will reduce if there was only good in them, so they almost choose the worst of what the world has to offer. I guess this is the irony that most news channels and gossip magazines thrive on – the human mind is attracted to drama of all kinds but particularly the negative variety. It feeds our ego, which loves this type of content and which in turn nurtures it to grow stronger.

How could I be sane in the real sense of the world? I have been programming my mind for years using newspapers, news and entertainment channels about what normalcy should be and here I am. After 30 strong years, I had landed a well-programmed definition of the state of the world. No wonder when someone asked me how I was, my answers usually ranged from "*Meh*" to "*It's OK*." Then, through the day, I remember feeling a sense of gloom. My body language screaming - "*what does it even matter what I do, the world sucks anyway.*"

And it's not just the external world at large: our close circle of friends also try to enforce an image of life as morose, tragic and sad. The unified vision of the world as programmed by the media reflects in most members of the society, who will radiate the same to us. They will make believe that life is largely tough and no matter what we do, struggle will be the way of life. It doesn't matter if it's a country or person, negative is the new positive.

Every day presents us with the options to choose what information we absorb: the choice is ours. For the first 2-3 hours of the morning, we are like an empty sponge. Our mind is rested and there is silence, as thoughts aren't all-pervasive in our minds yet. But what do we do? Right when our absorption is at its strongest, we choose to fill it with stories of insecurity based on physical appearance, failure in relationships or careers, heartbreak, rape and murder. Is it any wonder then that we often feel heavy, foggy, and restless, with an unknown sense of sadness that we cannot really point to?

But here is the trick. No matter how programmed you are currently to believe otherwise, we have complete control over what we choose to absorb. We can choose who we hang out with, the channel we watch, and the radio show we listen to. And most of all, we completely own the fact that we can walk out of any situation or conversation if it doesn't serve us toward our highest good. The Earth is an extremely loving and giving place. It's the people and their mighty egos that has manifested a reality of Earth that is so far from what it actually is. The world is positive, it's what we are doing with it that is not so much. In order to retain this positive view of the world, it is important to be cautious about:

- What we choose to see
- What we choose to hear
- What we choose to say

We each have a responsibility to uphold a vision of the world that reflects love, generosity and kindness. And we can do that by spinning out a positive feedback to the world where the information passing through the millions of terabytes of data is more positive and serves us at the highest level. We can choose to absorb and in turn send out the best form of information, each day and every day, through our words and actions.

I try really hard to be gentle to myself in the morning, as I am aware of my vulnerability in this hour. The first thing I do is to turn on some really calming music and read a few paragraphs of a great book. It just settles me in. I try only to absorb the good and refrain from anything jarring in my space.

But the space around us is our own and we can put the guardrails on what we choose to absorb, but we can't always choose what is thrown at us from outside our space. That's why it is important to choose the people we surround ourselves with so that we can have a level of control over the content we hear. We become the people we spend the most time with.

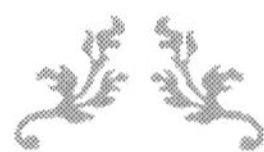

Takeaway

The goal is to stay away from rage, frenzy and negativity. We easily become what we absorb, so why not choose to be the best version that we can be? But for that we need to absorb the best of what this world has to offer. Being selective of what we soak in day-to-day and the people who influence our lives is incredibly important for our overall emotional and physical health. Don't let the complexity of other people and the world at large throw your balance off.

Moment of contemplation:

Have the happenings of the world changed your attitude? How?

What makes selective absorption of content rather difficult in your life?

____

____

____

____

"I want to be in love but . . ."

"But what?"

"It seems so tough and needs so much work"

Falling For Love

"We fall in love by chance, we stay in love by choice."

~Anonymous

Dear P,

I had a propensity to fall in love. Constantly. Or whatever I understood love to be. Starting in the early years at 13, my heart melted very soon and very often, much to the dismay of my parents and myself, because it impacted me in many different ways. I have seen many different facets of love. From peeking hard through the window to catch a quick glimpse, finding an excuse to accompany someone on the way home, writing someone's name again and again on a piece of paper, to choosing majors to be with someone in the same class. On the other side of the coin, I have also seen molestation up close in the name of love as well as serious stalking and mental abuse. Needless to say, love is a potpourri of different events and experiences. It's uplifting and downtrodden, joyous and menacing. When we bring love into our lives, we have to know it's not one consistent serene path but a twisted road to self-discovery.

I met this guy when I was all of 15. We met, liked each other, hated each other, loved, fought, cried, and have stayed together ever since. People call me lucky to have had a love so strong for so many years, and in many ways I am. We are. But love is life itself. Just like life is a journey where you learn, unlearn and at the end come out with wisdom, love is no different. We go through periods of intense learning, creating patterns and prejudices about each other, discovering nuances in the other and ourselves. We realize new truths, then unlearn the programs we built around love and build new programming. We may go through many rounds of unlearning, until we realize we are at the very center of it all. There is nothing more to peel and we are finally looking truth in the face.

Once we have had our fun and games, we can't help getting to know ourselves a lot better. Our relationships become the cornerstone of our life by being a mirror to our own self. We do unto others what we do to us. We judge others the most wherever we judge ourselves the most. In many ways, our most intimate relationships bear the harshest brunt of our journey of self-discovery. We can't stand a less than perfect partner, because we see a reflection of everything in us that needs work.

Probably the hardest part was learning that both of us are on a journey of our own, and it is essential we don't take away that space or permission from each other. All relationships are spiritual in nature as long as the intent of starting them is noble. More often than not, we just give up on most of them before the realization hits home. Drama, anger, jealousy – all our ego-based behaviors take over and we begin to lose those battles.

As we respect a relationship and nurture it with patience and kindness, love holds the space for the relationship to grow. It self-perpetuates as it feeds on our patience. At some point, there is almost a certain resonance, a tipping point, where we as individuals rise so high in the relationship that it becomes the wind beneath our wings, propelling us higher in all parts of our life – health, finances, career, you name it. So, perfection is a foolish idea to look for in a partner. If the person has no regions for growth, they are as good as dead. Why live if there is no need to evolve?

So, are you looking for that perfect person for yourself? How was that perception created? Books, movies and friends talking about their perfect halves? Love somehow gets lost in all of this. It's unable to stand up against its biggest nemesis – the perception of being perfect. Because love is the quieter one, less conspicuous, it speaks less and does more. It's a constant battle which perception could have always easily won, if only perception was not so vain.

Love always comes through: it's the anchor that fights for you through the worst storms. It wins because it's pure and honest. Love is indeed the choice we make. The choice can be hard, since the first impression of love doesn't sweep the ground away. It stands at distance and looks out for you. But the choice is rewarding. It's a reward for you to have chosen honesty over vanity, the prospect of long-term happiness over a few adrenaline rushes.

But here is the fact plain and simple – relationships take work. Accept it and move forward. When things are not quite right, there is some change involved for good reasons. When people say relationships take work – well our lives take work, don't they? Here we are talking about sharing our life with someone who in their own way is working on their life path – why wouldn't it take work? But what I have realized is that the work relationships take is majorly the work we do on our own self. To stop judging someone constantly for a particular thing, we need to change something fundamental in ourselves. So, even though it may seem that we have worked on the relationship to accept something about our partner, we have changed a programming in ourselves. That's huge! Love is the space holder: all the growing, evolving, learning happens in that space.

My greatest success in this lifetime has been to find a lifelong friend in my partner. The peace in such a thing is humongous. It allows me the space to cut out from a lot of other areas and focus on my creativity. If I was always preoccupied with my emotional imbalance, I would not be doing the things that bring me so much joy every day. To share this lifetime with someone with an open heart is a precious gift that I don't take lightly.

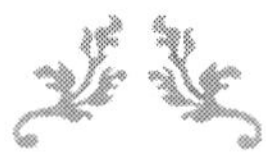

Takeaway

Give that love some time and space. Don't rush it. Because even though it seems like you may be wasting time and it's a ton of work and all you see is the difficult nature of it all, the person came into your life for reason. And every time we struggle with a habit or idiosyncrasies in our partner, let's take a minute to look within. The interesting question is, which picture within you is it knocking and what is really causing the discomfort?

Moment of contemplation:

Describe your ideas about love.

What has left a mark from all your previous experiences falling in love?

What is one pattern that keeps repeating in all your relationships?

"I have so many problems. How do I solve them all?"

"Why do you have so many problems?"

"I wish I knew."

Solving by Detaching

"You cannot solve a problem with the same mind that created it."

~Albert Einstein

Dear P,

The most ubiquitous word that gets etched in our life dictionary through the teen years and beyond is 'problems.' Everyone seemed to have a minimum of one but an average of many. The trend caught up with me soon enough. My late teens were a barrage of medium to large to really large problems. They come in all sizes and they insist you try them on. And then they stick to you! A large part of my time and life were spent figuring out how to solve these problems. They ranged from not getting along with my parents, to boy issues, to friends not giving me attention, to dealing with larger domestic issues at home. For the longest time, life's sole existence seemed to be this rigmarole of finding a problem -> experiencing grief -> solving the problem -> back to finding a problem.

In fact, I thought that grief was the default emotion of life and staying morose was the thing to do. Yes, I am not kidding about this: I remained sad for most of my teens and a better part of the early 20s. I was really good at finding a problem and experiencing grief. Really good. It's the solving of the problem where I struggled the most, and part of me did not want to, either. I had this amazing penchant to hold onto every situation that caused a problem.

This world is not short of things that can put you off. You need to get into a bad situation, have at it. You need a person to tick you off, have a hundred. Not surprisingly, I found myself in many hurtful situations. My heart would get so heavy that I couldn't function anymore, but I was reluctant to give in. Pride was at stake! I wanted out, but could not seem to figure out an exit strategy.

I felt captive to that moment, to the situation, the person. There was a strong resistance to seeing anything but the moment when the words were said or the things were done. I played the scene over and over again in my mind, and with every replay, the feelings grew stronger. It was like I was fueling the despair by fanning it. My focus was doing nothing but making the very thing that I wanted to get rid of even stronger.

Much later in my 20, I learnt the miraculous practice of detachment. I realized that constantly sitting amidst the drama was not helping me look at the situation objectively. It was imperative for me to step out for a bit and take a different perspective. I started a new practice called "going to the dark theater".

I close my eyes and imagine that I am sitting in the audience in a dark theater. The lights are all focused on the stage. I then play out the entire situation I am dealing with from beginning to end like a movie. It is important to manage my temptation to bias the play to beef up my end of the story and to really stay objective about the way it happened. I just look at it as an audience with no stake in the movie and with no attachment to any characters in the play. I become the watcher. After some initial discomfort, with practice I got really good at creating the separation. It is hard not to come out of this exercise without greater insight about the situation, if you have participated in it honestly. I would usually just get my answer during the exercise. Most of them were omnipresent from the very beginning and I just needed validation.

The next part was harder for me. What do I do next? Especially when I had to take the next step toward the resolution. Acceptance is key here, and it was vital for me to take responsibility for my actions and do what needed to be done. *Do I need to forgive someone? Do I need to ask someone for their forgiveness? Do I just need to acknowledge that I didn't choose my words wisely? Is there too much pride involved? Do I need to just remain silent? Do I need to stand up for myself and tell the facts*? Once I had a next step and the required gumption to rise above the ego traps to actually take that step, the persisting problem would just magically diffuse.

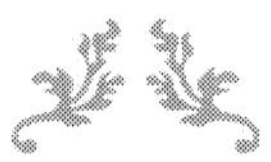

Takeaway

Life is a never-ending saga of relationships and situations. We get entangled in our lives so much that we forget that we are not these characters that our ego creates. We are not the center of the universe. Looking at these characters as a detached audience creates a space where we can dis-identify ourselves from our ego. It has taken me a long time to reach the realization that I am not the girl who insulted or hurt someone, or was insulted, hit, bullied, harassed, or molested – that is not who I really am, even though I experienced these feelings or are experiencing them in present time. That is not me! I am the awareness who is watching all this happen in the human realm and is inherently peaceful in nature. If we created the problem with our ego-self, we cannot solve it with the same. Detaching ourselves from the mind-based story helps us to experience the difference between our ego-self and the truth of us as a divine soul and leverage that authentic power. We are gifted with incredible wisdom and the power to own the reins to circumstances in our lives. This is gold for those times when we are in a pickle, not just in adolescence but in all of life.

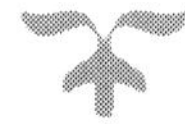

Moment of contemplation:

Pick a problem that's been troubling you. Practice "going to the dark theater" and play out your situation. What did you find?

What steps can you take to remedy the situation?

___

___

___

___

"I am in a relationship."

"What does that mean to you?"

"I now have him for me forever. I will never be alone."

Relationships that Nurture

"Don't settle for a relationship that won't let you be yourself."

~Oprah Winfrey

Dear P,

A large part of our lives is about relationships. Human connection is an important part of our ethos and there is no question that it makes life worthwhile. There is no beginning or end to when we start forming relationships, but at any point in our aware lives, we are usually in the midst of multiple relationships which are at various levels of intimacy and familiarity.

In my experience, there are two kinds of relationships we keep while in the world– there are those that you feel a pull for and those where you need to push yourself to participate. Most of the time, our lives are a mix of push and pull relationships and some that are between the two. Needless to say, I have had a good share of both types.

The push ones are characteristically inorganic in nature. They may start off on a good note but there seems to be an agenda underlying the foundation of these relationships. There is an understanding that the relationship will give rise to other openings and opportunities for the parties involved. Sometimes, there is an intense physical attraction or submission to a compromise for someone else's happiness. The uneasy thing about these relationships is in fact the uneasiness around them. Significant effort is required to keep them working. But more importantly, we can feel the effort in our bones. There is an indelible misalignment that we feel around them, and although we cannot put a finger on it, there is a constant feeling that something is not right, no matter how much we want to shove that feeling aside. Truth be told, we are not ourselves in these relationships, and are being stretched like play-doh just so we can fit into the pictures that we share of how we should be to make the relationship work.

Then there is the other kind. The pull ones have simplicity around them – you meet someone once and you feel, "Ahhh." Our breathing slows down and there is no effort involved. We feel like we can just sink in our seats and rest our backs. Feelings of liberation, belonging and oneness pervade our body and stay. Our body feels safe and nurtured. These relationships may involve fights, challenging conversations and disappointments, but never an expectation to fundamentally change into a different person. They provide us a sense of detachment even in the midst of a most beautiful attachment. Most importantly, the relationship creates a space to allow us to be who we are. This space, as I see it now with the worrisome adolescence behind me, is supremely important for exploring our faculties and growing into who we are – as an individual and as a participant in the relationship.

The push and pull dwell within us as well. Our relationship to our own selves plays out in the center of the other relationships of our lives. Growing up, I pushed to change myself to fit into an idea of who I should be. All the while, I wanted to pull my own true self and bring it to the forefront. As a young adult, I ignored one for the other so that I could fit into social pictures that were shown to me from my very early childhood – what I should wear, who I should hang out with, what my mannerisms should be, what I should like and dislike, etc. I played along while part of me just knew who I was and that everything else was someone else's idea. I believe a lot of the complexity of adolescence is a result of this tug of war within us. As long as we remain uncertain of this relationship with the self, we will be sending out confusing signals around the kind of relationships we want to establish. We will attract the wrong people into our lives consistently.

The same stands for relationships with places where we work or volunteer. I love going to work because I can be my whole self without putting on a 'workday' mask. My mentors, managers and peers experience and appreciate the same 'me.' But this was not always the case. I found myself always in the wrong jobs, doing things I did not like, attracting the wrong kind of office chatter. It was time to look within. It was because of the multiple professional masks I was wearing that people didn't know who I was, what I really liked to do. I now surround myself with projects that complement my true self and clients that bring their authentic selves to work and respect me for bringing my own.

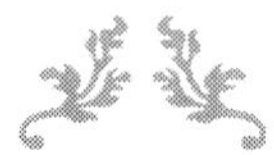

Takeaway

I realize that time is running out and with the current uncertainties in world affairs, I see no reason to not be who I am; and absolutely no reason to dwell on relationships that do not nurture me and appreciate me for who I am. I realize the investment of my time (and money) is best spent in listening to and nurturing myself and then relationships near and far. If this idea is selfish to me and others, I remind myself that all the malice in the world starts from us denying ourselves the permission to discover and align to our own individual self and then pushing the cart through the precipice by participating in relationships with a well-made false self that cuts the placenta with the universal life all together. If we are misaligned within, we can never be at peace in our external relationships. If you are wondering why you land up with the same kind of relationships which push you in a direction where you don't feel good, look within. Charity truly begins at home. We owe ourselves the highest love. And that means acknowledging that we are deserving of the best – from ourselves and others.

Moment of contemplation:

Think of the top three relationships in your life. Do you think they are push or pull relationships?

What kind of a relationship do you have with your job? Push or pull?

____

____

____

____

"Have you traveled to a new place lately?"

"I am so busy with school and work. Where is the time?"

The Spirit of Travel

"Something hidden. Go and find it.

Go and look behind the Ranges.

Something lost behind the Ranges.

Lost and waiting for you. Go."

~Rudyard Kipling

Dear P,

I was a homebody. Staying grounded in one place was my thing. My home was my world and the learnings of life were within the bounds of my home. I had marked the territories very clearly and wanted to stay within the confines of what was comfortable. People, places, things were analyzed characters in my head. There were boundaries, notions, ideas around each. I always thought people had to have lost their mind to spend resources to go to a faraway place. I was so wrong about that.

Living vicariously through other people rather than packing my own bags had its roots in laziness and fear of the unknown, and part of me knew that. There was a fear of not knowing what the land could offer me, and then there were the well-socialized thoughts: "*The people there are different!*" "*The country is not safe.*" "*people are known to be rude here.*" If I wasn't familiar with a place or the people, it must be bad or scary.

This was the case until I made my first international trip. And as clichéd as it may sound, it changed me forever. I couldn't fathom how people in a faraway country would help me for no reason when I had lost my way or needed help maneuvering through a new city. Or that they would be so like me. That they would smile even though they didn't know me.

My mind was blown. I spent some time pondering on the impact of my first faraway trip.

Our minds prefer a myopic view of the world; that way, it has a more manageable set of patterns to play with. It likes to work with a limited sample of data so that it can skew and bias our analysis of the world. Traveling and exploring invites many new possibilities into the mix, and in the process gives us a more holistic view of the world, unbiased and not limited to heresy. But deep inside, all of us remain explorers. We want to get lost in the woods, in the thin air of the fierce mountains, in the mystery of the northern lights; to find the valleys within ourselves that can only be witnessed when we are humbled by how small we really are.

I have since traveled to multiple places in Europe and the Americas. Travel has been the default bucket for all our entertainment savings. We have consciously cut down on restaurants and other extra spend buckets so we can put all the eggs into travel. My travels have taken me to places where I went in with some level of prejudice, mostly from the news and social talk. In every case, I have come out with a different perspective, mostly enlightening and always enriching. Traveling have changed my approach to countries, cultures and people. But most importantly, it has given me the perspective that we are all inherently the same.

Traveling is not always about the laurels we collect upon uploading pictures to our Facebook account to garner likes; it's more rooted in its benefits than that. New surroundings, people, cultures, food, sceneries open our mind and heart to new patterns of thinking. It challenges us to look beyond our own and extend our "hello" to something beyond the familiar ... I have experienced awareness and presence in a whole different way when I am in a new place – mesmerized and in awe, and at other times it's the need of the hour if I am hiking a mountain. Some places on the planet draw you in a different way altogether: it feels like déjà vu. There is a sense of completion when we visit these places.

We grew up learning that we are separate from each other and that survival of the fittest requires us to be different, superiorly different from the other. Exploring other parts of the world and meeting people from different cultures starts to scrub out the notion of separateness. Every culture has its idiosyncrasies and customs, but once you go beyond them, we are all the same. We need this awareness to save this world from wars and infighting. Imagine a world where everyone believes others are no different from ourselves, and what affects us affects the other person equally. Pretty miraculous! And of course you can't forget the feeling of the awareness that we are so deeply alive when we are one with nature and the gratitude we feel to be part of this stunning and awe inspiring ecosystem.

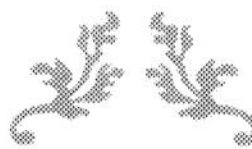

Takeaway

Pack your bags and go! Go and find it! That 70" television set can wait...

Moment of contemplation:

What are three new places you have traveled to in the last year?

What did you learn from those travel experiences?

What preconceived ideas have been debunked by your past travels?

____

____

____

____

"You know, when I brew my tea, I feel so at peace."

"What is it about brewing tea you think?"

"I think it's just a personal space where I can be wholly myself."

Rituals that Anchor Us

"Life's roughest storms prove the strength of our anchors."

~Anonymous

Dear P,

As a teen, I would be extremely busy through the day, but when twilight arrived, I would quieten down and spend time just staring out at the scenery in the beautiful background of black and blue. It was my favorite time of day. I remember earnestly waiting for the time, and it would come every day, rain or shine. It reminded me that all was well with the world no matter what happened in my own day. Much later in my life, I realized that this time of day acted as an anchor for my life.

As a newbie to the corporate workforce, I developed a ritual of brewing chai every evening. No matter how the day went, I would look forward to that time of the day. I would give up on highly popular after-work drinking sessions to just be home for this time. When I got married, my husband and I looked forward to the time of the day when I would brew chai and we would sip for it for an hour, talking about the day and life in general. It was a sacred time, much like twilight when I was growing up. I would not compromise on it for anything.

I also developed smaller rituals throughout my life, like lighting a candle while writing or praying every day for a minute or checking on my breath when I am angry or tense: just being aware would calm me down. Opening the pages of my journal to write has always been a homecoming where I just know I will connect with a higher source when I indulge in it. I have friends who have the same relationship with their yoga practice or painting at a certain time of the day, or their morning coffee time.

Anchors have a subtle way of appearing in our lives. They are rarely established with effort. They are an organic part of our lives, and for some reason they happen every day, much like a habit but not really one. They do more than meets the eye. They ground the fleeting nature of everything around us by being consistent. We anchor around them because they create a safe space where we can be ourselves. I imagine myself as a boat in fierce waters with these anchors all around me, keeping me safe. Even though I sway in the waters, I feel a sense of being OK. When I have had a rough day, I come back and brew some tea, and in the act of the ritual, I find myself more in my body. In many ways, the rituals are meditations that our lives have chosen to have in this lifetime. I have also found that once developed, they never leave us. Habits can change but rituals stay on: they have a higher purpose in our lives.

How we do develop these rituals? I have no real clue, but maybe by being curious about the things we like and in that process some just stick forever. It's recognizing the inner propensity to things/activities/people that makes us feel whole. We cannot develop them: either we find them or they find us. We don't nurture them, because again, there is effort in nurturing. Rituals don't need our effort, they need our participation, or shall I say, they enjoy our participation.

Takeaway

Honor rituals that bring you joy, where you can be your authentic self. They create a grounding chord to our crazy life and help us align to the source energy part of us, even if it for fleeting moments.

Moment of contemplation:

Describe key rituals you have developed in your life

What do these rituals bring to your life?

How does missing these rituals make you feel?

"Sometimes I feel a strong voice. It tries to send me a message."

"Do you pay heed?"

"Not really. I am not so sure about what I am hearing,
the legitimacy of it all."

Respond to Those Quirky Messages

"A gift is pure when it is given from the heart to the right person at the right time and at the right place, and when we expect nothing in return."

~Bhagavad Gita

Dear P,

Ever have a nudge, sometimes even nagging? We usually consider it to be a passing thought. But it is not. Arising from nowhere, but somewhere very close to us, we hear it loud and clear. We do but we don't. It's not always clear why we hear what we hear. We humans fundamentally like validation before we take anything seriously, and thus a message with no legitimacy of source is bewildering to us. What do we do with the message? Is it a passing thought like the 5,000 others that just went through in the past 5 minutes alone? Or is it something more?

Call it intuition, or the fact that all humans are psychic, or that our true self is connected to a deep pool of wisdom – nudges and intuitive messages are communication mechanisms that may be hard to scientifically prove through a theory. But I have found that practicing the art and therefore validating the sincerity in the messages has been fascinating for me.

I was all of 16 at the time, spending my days in a boarding school hundreds of miles from home. Walking down the usual busy street, I suddenly experienced a strong pull. A homeless woman with two kids was sitting across the street from me, begging for some pennies. For those of you who have never been to India, sights like these are very common and you soon learn to completely ignore the ubiquitous presence and their desperate requests very instinctively. But that day was different. I felt drawn to them. It was like something inside of me was begging me to help them. I felt stupid, but the voice was so strong that I had to respond.

I bought a bottle of milk, bread and some cookies from a store nearby. Walking across, I was full of trepidation about how they would react and completely surprised by my own reactions. I felt possessed by something greater than me. When I handed over the stuff to the woman, one of the kids on her lap gave me 'this' look. He had probably not seen food for a few days. That look was something far beyond what I can explain with my vocabulary here. It was a look that could manifest all of humanity. I had never known community, compassion and love the way I knew them in that moment. Such a cliché, but it changed me. Whatever I am today, whatever I might become, the reason I am writing these notes in some way or another goes back to that moment: the moment where I felt completely connected to a higher realm, where I saw God in the eyes of a child, and I felt a serious alignment with the universe, where I was asked to trust something intangible. But what if I hadn't listened to that voice inside me that day? What if I never had the moment? What if?

The unseen dimension of a human life has a clear connection to a higher wisdom. Most of the time, the busyness of life keeps the connection just loose enough so that we do not make it primary in our lives. Our minds cannot fathom the vastness of the human spirit and thus cannot trust it enough to respond. It's not pragmatic to make decisions based on a nudge or a gut feel. We cannot process them because social conditioning says that in order to come to best decision, we should deliberate, consult, and deliberate more. It cannot possibly be a whim that arrives in our laps.

The truth is that it is. It has taken me a long time to realize that my best decisions come out of a small nudge that asks me to stop and reassess, pause, not make a decision, not right now, or plain and simple, don't do it. Once I really started thinking about my intuitions, which is ironic, it's astonishing how clear the messaging really is. The learning for me was to be more receptive to the voice of my soul. There was a realization that my soul does not understand ego, it does not understand that someone can be less than or greater than me. It comes from the world of love, and that is its only expression. Since then, I have had several quirky messages come to me, including some bizarre ones like giving someone my coat, paying for someone's train ticket, complimenting someone, an instinctive need to call someone – all of these messages have come to me out of nowhere. And I responded to the extent I could in those situations, and I am better off for it.

My notes are not about proving my viewpoint by referencing research papers. There are other books for that. This entire compilation of notes is based on a nudge that I received that writing this or creating this compilation was very important. I had and still have no idea of how important or why, just that it was important, something that I ought to do while I am alive. In that respect, nudges are asking us to take notice of our alignment to our higher selves at all times. As expected, I thought it was an extremely stupid idea. Why would anyone want to read notes I have written to myself? It just did not make any practical sense. I made tons of excuses – *everyone is too busy to read stuff like this, I am so busy, maybe in a few years.* The power of the messaging grew substantially over time as I kept ignoring it, to the point that it was all I could think about, day or night. I tried to tune out the messages. When I did not pay attention to the urges, I felt deeply misaligned, like something was not right. Thankfully, my internal compass kept course, correcting me as long as I listened.

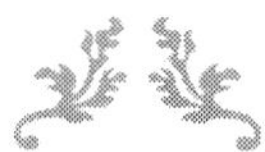

Takeaway

Responding to the nudges and intuitive messages that come to you will behoove you to go out of your way, go above and beyond, and do all this while the bigger picture is not yet clear to you. It is an act of pure surrender and trust in the mechanics of life, and thus the rewards are high, not necessarily in the form of money or fame, both of which are great, but something more intrinsically fulfilling. I am talking about pure joy. The joy of aligning to a higher self that is elated by the harmony of the body, mind and spirit. And that joy cannot be articulated or shared. It's when you just smile because you know. You *know.*

Moment of contemplation:

What intuitive messages have been appearing in your life?

If applicable, what is making you resist paying heed?

"I just had to say it to her. She was so mean."

"How do you feel now that you have said it?"

"I am not so sure."

Rethink that Quick Response

"Be careful what you say. You can say something hurtful in ten seconds, but ten years later, the wounds are still there."

~Joel Osteen

Dear P,

I was a feisty little one. I was always up for a fight, a quick response. Tit for tat was such a big part of my social environment while growing up, I couldn't imagine not responding back. Through the years, I encountered many moments where people hurt and diminished me with their words. Oh, there have been so many of those that it's not even funny! I quickly established that this is the way the world works. People are hurtful and ungrateful and I have to give it back to them. Otherwise they will not learn. Not responding to slights is an indication of weakness, and to keep my standing in the universe (read society) as a powerful girl, I need to come back with a vengeance. I am not an aggressive person by nature, but I cannot stand someone looking down upon me, and the least I can do is stand up for myself. Over the years, I executed many such backhanded responses with élan! And for a second, the moment feels very powerful. I would feel my chest rising and then pretty soon after ... diminishing. The feeling was so quick to fade. Every time I indulged in these quick responses, I found myself drained of life energy. I would also subtly realize that I just contributed to making the world a little bit more negative.

After the initial pride faded, I was left depleted, to the point that I could not be myself in other areas of my life. Sometimes, I felt that I was constantly looking for opportunities to respond back, maybe because I was addicted to the two-second high. The anger within was seething and the responses sometimes came too soon for my own good. There was no judgment in them, just plain anger. Looking back, would I change anything in my response. Hell, yeah! I would!

I would replace the quick response with a slightly different approach. Wait. Take three deep breaths and watch myself breathing in and out. Block myself from all other thoughts for those moments and be completely present. Disentangle from the situation and remove myself such that I can watch it from a distance. And then let the words come through ...

This allows for our intelligence to talk instead of our thoughts or our ego. All this time we have let this ego talk and she has done her job. But we are vastly more intelligent than that. The real I has complete understanding of the perspective of that moment. It knows that the person who hurt me is hurting themselves. It knows that the best thing to do in that very moment of conflict is to say I understand, or just walk away. Or I may decide to say something anyway.

Let the real you represent you in these moments, not that crazy ball of momentum that just knows butting heads is the best solution to all uncomfortable situations in life. You will find yourself walking away from a situation, sometimes with a smile. Because you will know that it really, really does not matter.

Takeaway

When you don't have an answer, breathe. When you have one, breathe some more ...

Moment of contemplation:

Think of a moment in your life when someone said harsh words to you. What changes did you feel in your body?

How did you react?

How do you wish you'd reacted?

"She is always busy."

"So what?"

"I feel insecure, I feel like she is moving much faster than me."

Are You Busy?

"It's not enough to be busy, so are the ants.
The question is: what are we busy about?"

~Henry David Thoreau

Dear P,

At 27, I stumbled upon a curious phenomenon. I found everyone around me complaining about being busy. Ask a casual "*how are you?*" and the responses ranged through "*been better,*" "*work is super busy,*" "*Crazy busy.*" There is a tinge of amusement as I write this. But I do remember feeling left out of this curious world of crazy busyness, wondering why I was not as busy, or should I be busy all the time in order to be successful?

Unfortunately, busy is perceived to be synonymous with success in today's world. After learning more about this phenomenon, I realized it is an art. But it does not take more than just some good ol' common sense to know that people who are busy are one or more of the following:

- Cannot manage their time well
- Are really not speaking their truth
- Cannot say no
- Want to be known as successful and important
- Are not to be modeled

After some initial internal resistance, I aspired to never be busy. The experiences of my life are of my choosing. If that means I am overburdened by commitments – I chose it that way. If I am not purely lying about my life being busy, I am saying that I have taken on a lot and I cannot prioritize it, leaving me frazzled and ineffective. When I say I am busy, I send out a vibration that I do not have space for new things to come into my life. The universe responds with just that. If you find yourself busy enough to say just that I would encourage you to replace "*I am busy*" with "*I am easy.*" The vibration changes immediately and suddenly we have more room. Or ask yourself, "*Why am I busy?*" "*What have I recently taken on that is overwhelming me?*" and "*Why did I take that on?*"

We are all looking for edification from the world that we are worthy of the things we have to managed to purchase and the lifestyle we have chosen to pursue, even if we don't need them. "*I can't exercise because I am busy, I can't meditate for 10 mins a day, I can't sleep on time and get enough sleep, or I can't cook at home*" – busyness covers it all. If I am busy, I am forgiven of all the various excuses we make up in daily life.

Filling up our life with content is fairly easy, but filling it up with things that really matter is a different thing altogether. If our lives are choc-a-bloc with activities that bring us joy and alignment, we will be far from busy. We will be "easy" – rejuvenated and peppy. We may not have enough time to squeeze in a cocktail night, but our lives will be so full with energy that we won't need one. We humans are extremely fortunate that with every sunrise, we have the opportunity to get a period of time to be whoever we choose to be, and with every sunset we are reminded to do a review of the day. We have a limited amount of time in a day, a year, a life – choose the actions of the day wisely.

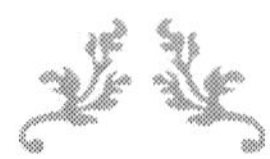

Takeaway

If we are busy, we need to stop and take a stock of every piece of clutter in our life and remove/eliminate as needed. Let's strive to stay away from the popular lifestyle of busyness – it's getting sort of old. It's a poor decoy for the ineffeciencies we have created and life creeps up on us sooner or later to call our bluff.

Moment of contemplation:

How do you feel when others say that they are busy?

Do you feel you are busy? If yes, then with what? Do you see any clutter in the day?

____

____

____

____

"She broke my heart again."

"Did she?"

"Yeah, she never lived up to what I expect of this friendship."

Mystery of Friendships

"True friendship comes when silence between two people is comfortable."

~David Tyson Gentry

Dear P,

It's an irony that we seek out friends throughout our teens but it's these friendships that cause us the most heartbreak. I remember fiercely looking for another person who in some way shape or form 'matched' me. Someone who was me but who I could actually speak to. I spent an extraordinary amount of energy managing and negotiating friendships. But as I look back at those years, I can see clearly what I was really doing. I was looking for people to provide answers, validate that I was liked and most importantly validate me, validate my existence on this planet. *Am I pretty? Too short? Will I ever amount to anything? Is it OK to be sad all the time?*

Sound familiar?

I met some extraordinary people who I fiercely guarded as my friends. Through high school, I went through a gamut of emotions with these handful of people – everything from extreme possessiveness to right out heartbreak. It's bewildering how much of our lives we invest in them. We want to be recognized by them constantly, not so subtly hinting *"Wrap me up in your blanket of friendship, protect me!"*

My high school best friend and I were fiercely close, more than sisters, as they say. For me, school meant her, and she was more than family. We shared so much of our lives, it felt like we would never be apart. Sadly, we had a major fall out after 10 years of friendship, which included a plethora of drama – the physical fight, the mental harassment, the name-calling, the utter heartache with guilt and pain sprinkled all around. My whole life was consumed by 'the fight.' At the time, it felt like life was over and the pain would never go away.

But it did. That's what time and life does – *renders everything impermanent.*

Let me break something to you. The friends you have today and who mean the world to you may not mean as much 10 years down the line. You may still be in touch with them, even call them often, but it's extraordinarily rare that they will be a part of your day-to-day life. You will have memories, some great ones but that's where it pretty much settles.

I ended up having many other friendships in different phases of my life. The friendships became fewer but increasingly more meaningful. Do I talk to them every day? No, I don't. But I respect them as human beings and I am thankful for their presence in my life. After years of investing myself in this thing called friendship, what I have realized is that the best ones are when you enjoy the company of a few special people, all the while being completely certain of who you are within yourself: not someone who has her career, love life and all the other lives figured out, but who knows and owns what she likes and doesn't like, what her principles and values are, and has a certainty about herself that other people cannot shake under any circumstance. When we are no longer looking for ourselves in other people, when we can be present in their company, celebrate who they are and how we are ourselves in their presence – that's when the most special friendships thrive. They require no 'effort' to maintain or nurture. We pick it up from where we left off – they just bring their whole self and I do the same. Seems like the magic combination!

Takeaway

Don't let the drama of a friendship ruin the teenage years for you. Life is bigger than that and no one relationship should carry the burden of your expectations and, in the same token, expect you to change to fit a certain cookie cutter idea of a person. Keep a tab on whether you are searching for yourself in the other. No one can be the best version of you like you can. Do not seek perfection when you can't promise the same, because you can't. What feels like the end of the world right now to you, may not even cross your mind in a few years…

Moment of contemplation:

What importance does friendship have in your life?

How would you feel if you no longer had your friends?

What are your expectations of your close friends?

"What should I focus on? My love for writing or this job …?"

"Can you choose what you love more?"

"But these bills I need to pay…"

Ensure Your Financial Freedom

"A big part of financial freedom is having your heart and mind free from worry about the what ifs of life."

~ Suzie Ormon

Dear P,

One thing I was very clear about while growing up was to have enough money in my pocket to fulfill my desires. I visualized it so clearly, and I never really saw an alternate to it. I knew I was a person who would need a certain amount of money to be happy. When I was living off my parents' money, my desire for money was driven hugely by my desire to prove a point to me, to afford the best of what's out there. To prove that I was better than others.

It all changed when I was working 30 hours per week and in parallel studying to finish my grad program. I graduated in the middle of the crashing stock markets in 2009 and it was tough for an immigrant student to get a job. There were no jobs, rest alone jobs that would sponsor an immigrant. It took a lot out of me and challenged me to the core. But I didn't lose my vision of ensuring my financial freedom. There was no question or doubt about it. So when the opportunities presented themselves, I valued the circumstances and was grateful for them. My gratitude brought a different relationship with money. I wanted to earn so I could serve myself, and that included people in my life I loved the most. I was never a spendthrift but I wanted to be able to buy the books that I was finishing by the day, participate in workshops, buy online programs and surprising loved ones with their choicest gifts.

I was awakened in a special way through the hardships and it desired a connection. I was invited to explore spirituality. But it was not cheap. Learning healing arts or meditation in this country can be a bomb, as I experienced. And I don't say that to lessen the value they deliver. It was important for me to earn money in order to participate in life, with life, the way it wanted me to. In the process, I think my creative channels opened up, maybe because I was so aware of what I was being guided to do. I was always writing, but it took a more, not serious, but a 'different' turn. I felt I was writing physically from the bottom of my heart. I was working in the day and writing at night and in the middle, my job funded everything I needed to bridge the two activities – my travel to places I never knew existed, access to books of all sorts, meeting people like Wayne Dyer, who changed my life, and my education in clairvoyance and the healing arts.

Could I do all this if I didn't have a job? – No. And I will not kid myself about that. I have come across the dilemma of whether my job is fulfilling enough to continue, and every time I have contemplated that, I have been intuitively guided to continue participating because it holds the space to have everything else I have in my life, at least for now. I could hide that fact as long as I live, but it won't change the truth – my job and the resulting financial freedom I have experienced has been a cradle for all the great and life-changing things that have happened in my life.

Different cultures have different outlooks on the relationship between women and money. In Asian cultures, women tend to pursue an academic life passionately but that does not always culminate in to a job, for a variety of different reasons. In many cases, it is society and our own families; it can also be circumstances that forces us to make a choice, and we pick giving up our financial freedom.

If you are a person with a sense of creativity or you do not have an awareness of your creative side yet but feel a nudge that there may be something, it is important that you ensure a life where you don't have to solely depend on another person's income to survive.

One of the worst silent killers of a creative life is the feeling that you can't step out of the norm because it will affect the relationships that support us financially. We are afraid to speak up and are conscious, even embarrassed of our confidence, These feelings are conducive to giving birth to psychosomatic issues but not to opening up our creative lives. In my experience, creativity speaks to us when we have gone above survival. Until that time, our whole life focuses on the one important goal, to survive and live, and the creative channels, by choice, shut down so that they don't pose as distractions. In dire times, the human body is wired to light up our survival meridians whenever we can't meet our basic needs of shelter, clothes and food. After that is taken care of, we rise up to the upper chakras or energy centers of our body, which can open up the space that we need to nurture our creative lives.

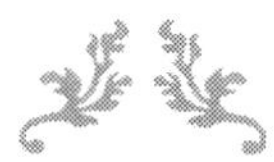

Takeaway

If creativity is what you desire, do whatever you can to ensure you don't depend on someone to pay your bills. It will kill it. Play at that bar, work at the subway, sell your paintings at smaller galleries, do that day job on the side that keeps your wallet warm. We may feel that it's consuming precious time, but as long as we keep our commitment to our creative side, I know we are helped by the powers that be to stay on the path.

Moment of contemplation:

Do you feel free financially? If no, what is holding you back?

If finances were not an issue, what creative projects would you take on?

___

___

___

___

"I keep dreaming."

"Dreaming is good."

"My dreams frustrate me."

Non-Committal Aspirations

"Some humans are born great and others achieve greatness,

But contrary to what Tony Robbins will tell you,

Most of us are perfectly content to have slightly above - averageness thrust upon us"

~ Mark Adams

Dear P,

A lot of us aspire to live great lives. Yes, we aspire. Aspirations can be authentically ours or just ego-driven thoughts that we harbor as our own. But either way, we are driven by them. There is something utterly soulful and romantic about ruminating about aspirations. As a teen, I harbored many such. I dreamt big. Images would rise up during school time and I would be transported into a whole different world.

Everything around me was an aspiration. The chic lady in the romance novel that I hid under my pillow or the successful CEOs in Forbes magazine, the uber successful TV stars, the authors whose books I devoured, my dad's words when he had a few pints of beer, and my friends and relatives – I was relentlessly presented with a dose of aspiration. There was a sense of knowing that there was still time left, but there was a dread that I might amount to nothing. There was just too much around me to focus on something specific and run with it. Perplexed and flustered, I just read my book in my small wooden room. I read and wrote to my heart's desire and let everything else sort of get into an autopilot.

It wasn't just me. I could sense people around me were all aspiring, looking into the future to see the big things we would achieve. As I grew up, although new aspirations sprung up, the old ones started rusting, tired of awaiting manifestation. Then before we knew it, aspiring but never realizing them became a pattern.

I believe that every aspiration that dawns upon us represents a certain possibility that we are capable of manifesting. When the muse hits us, our means and resources don't mean a thing; the resources appear if we take the aspiration seriously. And the scary part is that we, the truth inside of us, knows that with absolute certainty.

The irony of this story is the inherent propensity in us to never materialize aspirations. It's almost like we are scared, scared to make them come true. Unrequited aspiration seems better to our egos. They seduce us in a very interesting way. Struggles and challenges make for an interesting story. *Our greatest fear remains the possibility of success.* The change that will occur in our lives if we achieve success seems destructive to our minds.

But the bottom line of why I have avoided working on the multitude of callings that have visited me is laziness – being too lazy to act because 'aspiring' is easier than 'doing'. That's why I avoided exercising, eating healthy, working on my book, executing a plan for a great idea, leaving unpleasant jobs for the greater good of my life, etc. Eating a donut is always easier than doing 10 push-ups. Buying a domain and URL is easy; creating the content for the website is the difficult part. Creating a business plan for an entrepreneurial venture can be fairly easy; putting it to action is difficult. But we keep aspiring because we all know we can do the 10 push-ups, if we really try. We know what to do and why we should do it. But we don't. Because it's easier not to. We procrastinate about working on our aspirations endlessly until the aspiration is sick of knocking on our door and ultimately decides to leave and knock on someone else's.

I worked on writing my book for over two years. I was slacking considerably. *When I have more time … when work isn't as taxing … after I get married … after I have a kid.* The excuse production was creative. The draft would be lying across from me but I wouldn't work on it. More than laziness, it was the idea that I was shooting for something way bigger, and the understanding that as I put more time into it, I would have to keep putting in more time. What a way to think, but there I was in all my lame glory. I had to take responsibility for this creative work that was knocking the bezeeses out of me! It was dying to come out and it had chosen me as the nest to harbor and here I was, being the biggest procrastinator. I had to pick myself up from all the mind games and call a spade a spade. Aspirations seek respect. And I wasn't giving mine any.

Every so often, we blame circumstances and bad luck to camouflage our sluggishness to execute. Please avoid that trap. It's important to take control of our lives, and the teenage years form the basis to set the ground rules. At the very core, we all know we have the power to do anything, absolutely anything. We are scared of this phenomenal truth because once we take that in, that's it. It's like the universe is smirking back at us: "*what's stopping you?*" And we don't really have a ground-breaking answer. Our mind is constantly tricking us into believing that we can't achieve much of significance because of the hundred small excuses. Don't take your mind seriously. We need to push our limits that takes us beyond this natural reaction to aspirations. Victory of the self over the mind and the inconclusive reasoning on why we should not make it happen are necessary if meaning and purpose are things we hold dear.

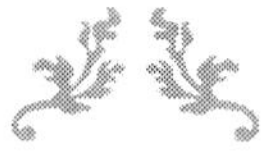

Takeaway

You are gifted such that many aspirations will come to you. Recognize your natural reaction of resistance toward them. At the same time, *know for sure, that you have all the components in the tool set to make the rubber hit the road*. And when it does, you will wonder, why, why did you wait so long?!? There are two things to remember:

- Get out there. There is only one way to stop procrastinating. Stop procrastinating.
- There is only one thing stopping you from achieving your goals. *Get yourself out of the way.*

Moment of contemplation:

What are three aspirations that you hold close to your heart?

What is keeping you from hitting the road with your aspirations?

"I have a deep desire to keep buying, like it never satisfies."

"Has anything ever satisfied you?"

"Yes, our conversations, listening to my favorite song…"

Embracing Experiences Instead

"The real voyage of discovery consists not in seeking new landscapes, but in having new eyes."

~Marcel Proust

Dear P,

As a teen, I was dangerously aware of the brands on my body and those on others. There was a mental ledger which was continuously doing debit and credit calculations on a person based on the number of brands on them. More frightening is the fact that almost everyone in my circle of friends had the same thought process. We had to fit in. We had to rise in the ledger. Sadly, stuff was the only worth I really understood. It didn't matter how many As I had; it mattered that I wore the right jeans.

When does it stop? Not soon enough.

The stuff keeps changing as the buying power changes, of course. We go from the jeans to the flat screen TV to the convertible. But the theory and the mental associations remain the same and the ledger stays handy. Instant gratification is honored time and again, and we relentlessly seek the possibility of changing the opinion of our friends about who we are with the things we possess.

What are we looking for? Have we ever stopped and listened to ourselves? We drown out any noise but the "I want," "I want," "I want" stays conspicuous. If we look a little closer, we are in fact looking for things that will define us, get us closer to who we really are. We are all fervently looking for ourselves in everything in our contextual field, in the relationships we have, in the movies we watch, in the food we eat and of course in all the stuff we possess. The truth is that we are constantly trying to find ourselves and we search for ourselves in these things.

The genesis of 'want' is in the longing to *know thyself.* Since the internal portals have not been opened yet, the external is the only playing field. Compound that with the survival of the fittest, and it's the perfect situation for us to race against others and ourselves to portray success. Even when we recognize the voice of the ego, we surrender to it, as the battle seems too huge to surmount.

Possessions are not bad: not bad at all. It's the association of stuff with self-worth and the eagerness to create a formula where the quantity of stuff is an integral multiplier of happiness – that's where the fallacy lies. A new possession helps to add another definition to who we are or to the idea of who we are. Needless to say, it's another wrench in our path to self-discovery. The external world can only give us a momentary high. The internal exploration is what leads us to more concrete answers to what we are looking for in these matters.

What can we do? Despite it all, it's very hard to be devoid of the urge to own more. It's hard not to give in. I stopped fighting it when I realized it's here to stay for a while. Ego is a real thing and we don't get up one morning and decide ego will no longer exist. So, I got my house, got my car, and got the stuff. But all the while, I was aware of the ego cropping up to drive me toward some more. I couldn't always help it, but the awareness was key to the realization that this treadmill will never stop. *Do I want to continue running on it, knowing the path it's going to take me on, or stop it and try another road?*

So I tried something new instead. I replaced the need for stuff with experiences. I started small. When I had a deep desire to buy something, I saved the money to travel to an unknown place, if I had enough time to go shopping then I spent it working on a short story or a book or made dinner for my partner or parents.

I realized pretty rapidly with the new approach that if happiness is the true index, my net happiness from the collected experiences was far greater than my collection of stuff. There is a certain sustained ecstasy, a rush when we are involved in experiences with people or nature. It's momentary, if not completely absent, when we buy something material to satisfy a craving. The rush spikes for a limited amount of time and then we move on to craving something else. The memories of an experience and how it made us feel stay with us no matter what.

Takeaway

It's not what we give but it is in the act of giving, feeling, seeing, helping where we see glimpses of our truest self. Maybe stuff exists so that we can give more, feel more, see more and help more, and in that process, explore the depths of our being, and maybe, just maybe, stumble upon our purpose and that thing called 'self'!

Moment of contemplation:

Indicate three things that you have bought recently that you thought would really have a big impact on the quality of your life.

List what differences you thought the three things would bring in your life.

Indicate how those things make you feel now.

____

____

____

____

"My job is sucking the life out of me."

"Do you want to look for a new one?"

"They all seem the same after a while."

What You Do Doesn't Matter

"I've learned that making a 'living' is not the same thing as making a 'life.'"

~Maya Angelou

Dear P,

I spent so much time trying to figure out what to do. And it's important to do that. Finding fulfilling work can change our life. And we need to do whatever it takes as we go through life to find the profession which resonates with us. But even when you find that fulfilment in a job, sustaining that feeling can seem like a struggle.

Most of your working life will be spent worrying about something that happened at work. Our workplaces become the center where we leave a lot of our own energy. We feel depleted when we return back home and try to get back our lost energy from the people at home – draining them in the process. Work becomes an enormously serious place and we can attribute a lot of our premature gray hair to it. The psychosomatic as well as physical changes it brings about by virtue of the stress and anxiety is usually gravely ignored.

What if I told you that at the end, it wouldn't matter if you are a project manager, a geologist or a gardener? When it comes to evaluation of life, if there is such a thing, it is simply how our life impacted other lives.

I have had the good and bad fortune of being a part of a few memorial services. These beautiful ceremonies are meant to celebrate the life of the departed. When friends and family come up to speak, there is no mention of their occupation or the titles they held. In none of those services have I heard someone say, "She did a great job as a director of so and so company," or, "he was an excellent Vice President at Company Y." They talk about their personalities, their quirks, their idiosyncrasies and how the departed soul impacted their life. Friends and family reminisce about how they were the life of the party, how they always listened – things that seem very day-to-day in our lives, but we realize how important these are when they are gone. It's amazing how in life and death, the value we attribute to things reverse so effortlessly.

My friend Gina was a special lady. We sat across from each other at work in Chicago for a year and became close friends. It's difficult to define Gina. She was weird, in a good way. Outspoken, fearless, authentic – she lived with her dog who she loved to pieces. From the outside, she lived a lonely life, but she always smiled and shared stories of her travel, strange encounters and varied experiences. At the age of 48, she was diagnosed with terminal cancer. She was in the hospice within five months of diagnosis. Death was imminent. She started a blog to write about her last few months on this planet. The posts were funny but more importantly indicative of her acceptance of the situation. She surrendered completely to the process of passing. At her funeral service, her friends and family spoke at length about what a wondrous thing her humor was. How it brought down the house. They talked about so many things that Gina did in service to others that I was completely unaware of. No one talked about what a great content strategist she was (which she was) and that she worked for big corporations, or any other detail of her resume.

The measure of life is really only about life. Our jobs may be a part of our lives but does not really qualify as life itself – something we lose sight of during the journey. We are all playing parts here. It's how we, including in our jobs, bring about a change in other people – that may be the game changer here! What you do really doesn't matter, it's how you touch others with what you do – that's the real deal. The impact of our work is truly the essence – *are we treating our colleagues and clients with kindness, making their life simpler with our solution? Are we humble in our successes at work that resonate with our peers in a very deep way? Are we able to lead and nurture teams and individuals without power struggles?*

Takeaway

We get consumed by the cycles of our jobs – from one promotion to the next, we feel we are being measured in life by our progressively increasing titles, and that we fail if we don't keep moving forward. This illusion about the true measure of life is frustrating and confusing. And to know that we only realize this for ourselves when we are dead or nearing it is truly a waste of life. So, next time when you get passed over for that promotion, instead of feeling dreadful and giving up on life, do something nice for someone in the office, mentor a junior or help a client out. When our life is being measured, the lost title will not feature anywhere, but that hour of kindness or that moment of service will never be forgotten and the impact will reverberate through the generations in unimaginable ways.

Moment of contemplation:

What comes to mind when you think about your job?

How do you think your work impacts others?

____

____

____

____

"I am constantly chasing life."

"Do you ever pause and look back?"

"There is no time. I am chasing my better self in the future..."

Don't Undermine Today

"If we do not feel grateful for what we already have,
what makes us think we'd be happy with more?"

~Anonymous

Dear P,

You know I think about my life a lot. But it is mostly about the future – planning for expected events and fear of unforeseen events. Where will I be in 10 years? What are my goals for the next two years? At 16, I was thinking about where I would be at 25. Would I be successful and would I have enough money to fulfill all my desires? At 25, I was such a mental mess, I wondered if I would survive the internal torture for another five years or just perish. I worked out so many of my fears and questions over the next two years – seeking teachers, reading everything to grow my self-awareness. By 27, I had a new-found peace that pervaded my soul, but I was invaded by the question of my purpose. What is my purpose? What am I here on this Earth to do? And I wondered whether I would continue to be flummoxed at 30.

Through it all, very seldom did I ever pause to think about how far I had come at the different stages of my life. There have been fleeting moments when a parent or an old friend reminded me of how confused I used to be and how sorted I seem now. My father would tell me over a glass of wine how proud he was, citing examples of how lost I was during my teenage years and then overcame so much adversity.

Sometimes my own processing of everyday issues surprised me. *How was I so poised?* Why didn't I feel bad? Or just recognizing ego when it crept up on me time and again: my growth thus far has been nothing short of fascinating when I actually put some thought to it. I am so much more aware of my faculties today than I was 10 years ago. Even when I am about to explode, there is that window of time when my consciousness has an emergency meeting with my ego about what my response should be. Even when I go ahead with the 'explode' option, I am at peace, since I know I made a conscious decision and that I actually had a choice.

I have been down and out at all stages – at 16, 25, 27, and 30 but I have risen. I have learnt more and more, even when I said I knew it all. I have loved and cared for people I know and people unknown. I keep digging deeper and deeper into my soul to know more about me and life as a whole. I am asking questions and finding my own answers. I have a semblance of understanding of the deep wisdom within me that I know I can go to whenever I need. I have an appreciation for humanity as we live through the complexities of a lifetime with the awareness that at the end of the day, the drama means nothing. It only means we have experienced newer things in this physical world. So, even if it is for a fleeting moment, I am going to applaud myself for who I have become and more importantly for who I am becoming.

I want to tell you that at 32, you will be just as wise as you were at 16. You just need to brush off more dust from the mantle: we are perfect when we are born and perfect when we die, it's just how much of the mantle we dust off through the process of life itself. Any effort in the dusting process is worthy of celebration, because that means we are going back to who we are originally – the godhead, the *atman*, the child detached from the body in the womb.

I am grateful for my journey and who I have come to be. I realize that there is something within me that is unchanging, but something else that's evolving every minute of every day. I salute both of those parts.

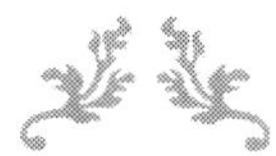

Takeaway

Pause. Pause now! Look at how far you have come. Pat your back. Being human is no easy feat. We live it and some more. The next 10 years can wait. This form of you, of me, this right here, this is what's most important.

Here is my prayer and request to you. No matter how hard life gets and how difficult it is to get through your day – *just know you have come a long way.* The road ahead will happen in its own good time. I am working on this little affirmation that I would urge you to make a part of your life as well …

"I am so grateful for who I am right now."

I say this when I wake up, just to remind myself that although there are things I am yet to learn, I acknowledge the learnings and the journey that have brought me to this moment. It's all within me now. It's all in who I am now. I am the sum of all of the moments in my life until now.

Moment of contemplation:

Describe a few things about yourself that you did not see 10 years ago but see now.

Take a few breaths and say the affirmation below. How does it make you feel?

"I am so grateful for who I am right now."

"Why don't you laugh more often?"

"I just feel like things need to be better for that."

Humor Yourself

"There is little success where there is little laughter."

~Andrew Carnegie

Dear P,

I was a pretty serious teen. I don't remember laughing that much. There were moments, though: moments of complete freedom where I felt like something within me just opened up and I became a different person – sharing a joke with a close friend, banter with my siblings or a humorous argument with my parents. I distinctly remember feeling very natural in my skin in those moments. As I grew up, those moments came more rarely. Life happened and I kept spinning. Life was a string of situations and experiences and I took them way too seriously. Each moment could either bring great embarrassment or great pride, very little in between. I am unable to look back at those days with great fondness. I remember being crazy busy all the time and maybe fearful of the future, but nothing more than that. But those tiny snippets of time where I laughed freely or shared a memorable joke with a friend stayed with me. How I wish I had had more of those …

I remember developing this strong prejudice about humor and laughter. I have no clue how I was conditioned to believe in them. For me, success and laughter did not go hand in hand. I had beliefs that if I was to score well in the exams, I should not indulge in laughter and humor, or if I was to be taken seriously at work, I should maintain a serious demeanor. I know, I know, I can hear you sigh, but I am putting my heart out here.

To top it up, life situations tended to appear far more important that they actually were in the bigger scheme of things. The truth is that whatever it is in your professional or personal life that you hold precious and you have this feeling that it is a matter of life and death – it is not! Let it go …

I realize I took myself way too seriously. My understanding of my role in my job and life seemed to be inflated in my mind. The truth is that the solar system we live in is a speck in the cosmos, of that the Earth is a tinier speck and I apparently am an important person in the cosmos?! No! It's hard to process, but the truth is that if I die, the world will go on, and although some will mourn, it will not make a dent in the workings of the world. It is high time I honor my precious life by smiling and laughing more often. I am a nobody. I never was and never will be. But my human life is tremendously special, as is everyone else's.

Life's very nature is to find its flow. It navigates itself just fine. What we mortals constantly try to do is to pretend that it won't navigate itself if we don't break ourselves to death or take it really seriously. Yes, hard work is the real deal, but struggle and worry are not.

Takeaway

Humor yourself today. Humor yourself every minute when you think it's getting pretty darn heavy. Release it. If that does not come naturally, try to smile more often, even if that's not your default. Nothing releases pent-up energy like laughter. Start filling up your 'moments' bucket from now: that's all you will remember. And try to find those special people who honor life with laughter. They rub off on us easily, and for once that's an infection I will take on at the drop of a hat!

Moment of contemplation:

What do you think about humor and laughter?

Do you feel like you have conditioned beliefs about humor? What are they?

Think of some people in your life around whom you smile and laugh more often. On the flipside, also think of the ones who tend to make you more serious.

"Sometimes I just want to feel something, anything."

"What do you do in response to this?"

"I eat, sometimes I fight with the people I love the most …"

Emotional Binging

"I don't believe people are looking for the meaning of life as much as they are looking for the experience of being alive."

~Joseph Campbell

Dear P,

I was 15 and stayed in a boarding school hundreds of miles away from home. Standing in a long queue at the boarding school café to get my serving of hot lentils and rice, it seemed like an eternity before I got a taste of them. Getting equal parts excited and angry, I would gobble up the food in an instant. It was almost like I breathed it down. This was the start of what was to be a pathological relationship with food. I would see a pizza in the hallway and a certain rush of getting free food, would sweep through me. I would also eat very quickly so that I ate unconsciously.

People advised self-discipline, but anyone who has gone through any kind of addiction knows, that darn thing is so hard to come by. The brain shuts down all logic and reason, so the focus is only on this savage need to eat the thing. The more reason tries, the greater is the desire to eat more.

I realized at 28 when I was 15lb overweight and borderline diabetic that it was time I put my hand on my mouth. But more fascinating was the realization that my binge eating had an important mission that I set for myself – that I needed to punish myself…every day!

Binging of any kind – whether it's watching TV, eating, drinking, spending too much money, getting into fights all the time, etc. finds its genesis in the anomalies of our relationship with ourselves. Somewhere, we haven't accepted ourselves for who we are. The resistance within looks for an outlet, and in the process, it encourages us to punish ourselves to the edge of the cliff. *"You are not good enough," "You don't deserve anything better," "You are worthless," "You are a failure"* – and we continue the addiction because at least there is something we can control.

For me, it was the desire to be skinny. I was never obese or remotely so. Instead, I have a rather muscular body because of years of rigorous swimming. I was ashamed of the muscles in my body. I kept dreaming of a slender body that never came. Every year that my body didn't change, I developed a burgeoning repulsion for myself. I showed my displeasure by eating wrong and eating a lot. The toxicity was palpable in my personality and it was a downward spiral that was moving faster than I could control.

To fix this situation, I needed a support system and a moderate will. If you get both, you lucked out. If one is missing, you have to up the game on the other or it's a bad fall. For example, I really struggled on the will part. So, my husband and I decided to not bring any junk or sugar-based foods home. He missed out on them, too, but he supported me through it all. I did have to say goodbye to socializing and frolicking to bars. With every disciplined step, I respected myself more. It was a slow process, but I could go back to my whole self again. I didn't repulse myself anymore which was a big win: instead I was blown away by my willingness to see this through.

Emotional binging is a reality. We cannot shove it under the carpet anymore. And people who experience this don't need sympathy but the empathy of friends and family. The long-term solution is to fix the root cause and not just the symptoms. I had to forgive parts of my life where I may have been bullied or criticized for my looks. I was also beware of those seemingly innocuous snarky comments from quarters close and afar. They do a lot of damage of a kind that can stay with us for a long time. I prayed for everyone who had words of criticism toward me, including myself. I had carried their hurting words with me for far too long. It was time I gave them permission to leave. I also resolved to never make a disparaging comment to someone else, no matter how funny it may seem in that moment. The human mind is complex and we cannot control its interpretations.

Takeaway

Addictions are far more common than you think and can sometimes sneak up on us. Identification and the decision to ride that out are paramount. Fixing the root causes can bring up periods of real darkness initially: that's why we need a support system. We need to be ready to meet this darkness head on if we want to lead this beautiful life without the consequences of addictions, which are nothing but negative thought patterns. This life is so precious and to pollute that based on past events and circumstances is, well, not worth it at all. It's time to lift the dark screen off your glasses!

Moment of contemplation:

What addictive patterns are you dealing with day to day?

What are the greatest barriers for you to get rid these addictions?

If you go back to your childhood, what was that one thing you were critical of yourself about? What led to you being critical about it?

___

___

___

___

"It's the same routine every day, exactly the same."

"What did you think it would be?"

"That it would be different."

Finding Meaning in Everyday Life

"Every day may not be good but there is something good in every day."

~Anonymous

Dear P,

Nothing surprised me more in adulthood than the truth about 'everyday life.' Age 12-22 is sort of a goal oriented life and every day counts toward this big kaboom waiting to happen when we grow up, when everything in life will be beautiful and you wake up in the morning jubilant with so much money to spend and so much happiness to be had! When you won't have to strive or struggle anymore and can just relax in peace. Getting through undergrad, grad school, getting a job – we are on the 'goal' drug that keeps us focused on this future goal. From when we open our eyes in the morning to the moment we hit the bed, we are overcome by this drive to get to that end goal.

Right about the time when I got my first job, I felt on the top of the world. The new people, the money in my account magically appearing every month, the laptop that a stranger just handed to me, the feeling of being of value – that stayed for a good month. And then one day, I got up in the morning with this sinking feeling. *The dread of going through the same drill all over again.*

I did not want to see the same people, work on this 'project,' look at the same Excel sheets or PowerPoint decks. Although situations at work varied, the structure of the day remained the same: Sleep-Shower-Work-Eat-Sleep. Talking to friends and colleagues, it was clear that they were particularly aware of the dreadful regularity of their lives as well. Life had turned out to be an anticlimax of sorts.

What I realized pretty quickly was that there is a taboo around socially acknowledging this, as this would mean we don't have fulfilling jobs or wholesome lives. But that is not true. I have come to realize that no matter how lofty the goal and how miraculously it was achieved, life plateaus if we are not chasing anything or striving to get to the next rung in the ladder. We expect our plateaued life to fervently replace the drug that drove us this far.

'Everyday life' is one of the greatest secrets about adult life that early education and our parents do a good job of keeping from us. We are just hit with it, and we have no clue what to do. Emotions run from boredom to suicidal, with some moments of joy sprinkled in between. But the joy is extremely fleeting and the boredom feels like it's here to stay. We seek excitement by partaking in social gatherings, entertaining people, going on vacation, going to bars and dousing ourselves in alcohol or worse in drugs. We are trying to get away from this dreadful disease called 'everyday life.'

After going through the phases of my own denial and the consequential depression, I had to look for another perspective. I challenged myself with an idea. How about treating every day as a canvas for experiencing our wholesome lives, like a lab for spiritual practice where we can bring our being-ness into each moment? Every day is a new combination of potions to be tested. Part of the reason we experience boredom in everyday life is because of the constant need to be somewhere else. If I can use my life to be in the moment, really surrender to what I am doing in that moment, at the end of that day, *it changes me*. It brings more of me to the table that I couldn't bring earlier. But I have to tell you, it's incredibly hard. So hard. That may be the reason why more people are fed up in the world than are not. It's a commitment that I believe we need to make every day, because every morning, when the sun shines and our eyes open, we have yet another chance to be more wholly us. What a privilege it is, and I have to remind myself that every morning.

The truth is that there is nothing more meaningful than 'everyday life.' There are countries in the world where people do not have the permission to have one, where the basic instinct is survival and seeing the sun shine is an anomaly since you are in hiding most times. It forces us to see more meaning, rattles us to be grateful and dig into the core of what a day in life is – truly a blank canvas. It can be whatever we make of it. It can be the most beautiful and also the most dreadful. Irrespective of circumstances, a day in life is largely how we feel, how present and grateful we are for the day. It tries to elicit that every day, nudges us to notice the stranger's smile or that piece of paper on the ground, or the fear that creeps up again while public speaking – what would you do about that today? It teases us to take notice of the moments that make the day and the ultimate power we have over our reaction to those moments.

I read the following Morning Prayer in the book *It's a Meaningful Life: It Just Takes Practice* by Bo Lozoff. It hit me in a powerful way and has stayed a part of my life since. Whenever I realize it is one of 'those' days, I remind myself to remember that this day, this 'everyday' day, could truly be my last.

I am a seeker of truth on a spiritual journey. I believe life has sacred meaning and purpose.
May my behavior today express my deepest beliefs
May I approach each and every task today with quite impeccability
May I be a simple, humble, kind presence on the Earth today
May I see the Divine Nature in all beings today
May I be grateful today to those who come before me, and may I make the roads smoother for those who will travel them after me
May I leave each place at least a little better than I found it today
May I truly cherish this day, knowing that it may be my last
May I remember, remember, remember, not to forget, forget, forget

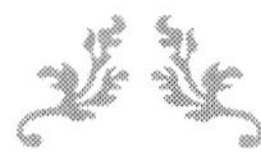

Takeaway

Presence is the only thing that will differentiate your days when the big goals have been met and the hurdles have been passed. If you feel bored or just lack meaning in everyday life, get quiet and be present. Do one thing fully present. It will change how you feel. Bring presence to something new every day, whether it's brushing your teeth or driving to work ... have fun with it!

Moment of contemplation:

Are you bored of the day-to-day?

How has routine affected your zest for life?

Is there an opportunity to do things differently in those routine activities of your everyday life?

III. TOWARDS COMPLETION

"How is life?"

"It seems full. Bloated."

Create Space for New Things

"Make space in your life for the inevitable arrival of what you want."

~Danielle LaPorte

Dear P,

As a teen, I had a pretty full calendar. Swimming, painting, classical dancing – I had a slot for every little thing out there. And when that lot was over, I was studying for exams. There was never a dull moment, and even playing was slotted into the day. The trend continued as time and life crept up on me. I continued the trend as a teen and young adult, with increasingly fewer punctuations through an eventful day. The events in the calendar kept changing, but the slots remained full. Looking back, I feel fortunate for the varied experiences, but I wish I had some time to take it all in and reflect on the impact the learnings from these activities had on my life, or to take time out and to consider which aspects of an experience I was enjoying the most or least.

We run from one thing to the other, with a pause to breathe if we are lucky. It is choc-a-bloc – make appointments, plan for the future, run businesses, etc. The calendar never stops getting filled up. And after a point, we are addicted to having no time. It's almost a matter of pride to be busy. It contributes to our social image by promoting the concept that if you have no time, you are probably successful! Hardly stopping to think about what we are filling up our days and years with, we are disturbingly content with having no time. Although we complain about the fact, secretly we are glad we don't have a dull moment.

When we look at our lives, we find that there is very little space for us to do *nothing*, when we can just be without having to justify the activity in the scope of our lives and feel the very life that we are – not a swimmer, a friend, a pianist, a writer. Just life. In the small spaces of nothingness, we have short glimpses of presence and a connection to a higher wisdom.

For musings and the muses to come to our lives, for divinity to pay us a visit, we need to connect to the rawness of life. And that does not always need us to relax atop the Himalayas. It only needs some free space so it can seat itself temporarily for at least a fleeting but eternal moment. If it knocks on the door but there is no space for inspiration to come in, it will politely move on to someone else who does have it. We need to create some space in our daily lives for life to be acknowledged. In the acknowledgment lies a recognition of the creativity that is in the ethos of this universe. Pausing from life creates moments where we can download higher wisdom from the special places.

I went through a phase of prolonged darkness in my early 20s. On the surface, everything was alright. College, friends and a vibrant social life were in motion, but deep inside I was dealing with anguish and disappointment, neither of which I could understand. While the reason for the darkness remained unfounded, I continued on a downward spiral. Not able to find a place where I could rest my mind, I found solace in self-reflection. Of course, I didn't know that's what I was doing, but journaling, walking and thinking about the questions arising inside gave me the space to purge the resentments and unforgiveness that I carried for myself and others. With the purging came a deep sense of relief, as well as room to explore opportunities, answers and ideas that came to me sparingly before.

What became clear to me was that the energy that doesn't belong to us prevents good things from coming to us. It's only when we sanctify our space, clear it off of unconscious energy, that's when we can welcome the transformative changes and events that are waiting to happen.

I started a more formal practice of running my energy and meditation in my late 20s that helped me to understand that as someone living this life day to day, I cannot expect a permanent purge, just yet. I need to clear energy every day because it piles up every day. Creating a ritual of flushing energy and creating a sacred space for the self is deeply essential for a fulfilling life. I use a technique I learnt in my training as a clairvoyant called 'grounding'. Just create an image of sitting on a tree trunk with its roots reaching the center of the earth. The seat of your spine should be connected to the tree trunk. Now set an intention of purging everything that is not your energy to flow through your seat into the center of mother earth who neutralizes any energy that's not yours, returning any energy that belongs to you. This is an abridged version of the practice. You can search for the complete version on YouTube or Google or look for a clairvoyant teacher in your area who can teach you the technique.

Takeaway

A quiet mind is a playground for God. It is a safe haven for creative inspirations to stop by and say hello to us. We may or may not pursue the commitment, but it loves to drop by in open and inviting spaces that have put in the effort to create the necessary quietude. Pause and take time out for reflection. Clear your calendar for doing nothing. It is as, if not more, important than doing something. And remove the clutter from your mind and life so great ideas and inspirations can make a pit stop!

Moment of contemplation:

In your everyday life, do you make space for yourself to do nothing? If yes, what impact has that time had in your life?

When do creative inspirations come to you most frequently?

____

____

____

____

"My friends like Duran Duran. I have started listening to them."

"Do you like them?"

"I don't know. But it's cool to throw their name into conversations."

Wear Your Authenticity

"Authenticity is the daily practice of letting go of who we think we're supposed to be and embracing who we are."

~Brené Brown

Dear P,

If there is one thing I have recognized from my growing years, it has to be the progressive elimination of authenticity in everyday life, from me and from everyone around me.

At 15, I had no idea who I really was. Every day was driven by my emotions and the happenings of life on that day. I would wake up and wait for the first tide of life situations to hit me. When the day was laced with drama, life was *busy and hard.* When the day turned uneventful, I identified it as *boring*.

As you might already know, there is a social mantle, a mantle of all things cool and the understanding is that we must try really hard to sit on that mantle. If we are not already sitting on it, then we are constantly in pursuit of it. We change and mold ourselves to get to the mantle. Not a lot of adults, especially parents, realize that one of the reasons that teens are suffering from depression and other confidence-related issues is because of this pursuit. Because that's what they know in order to count amongst peers and friends. And at that age, count we must. The parents are busy figuring out how to live with a hyperactive teen and are periodically looking at their own shining mantle with a centerpiece called "*How well are your kids doing?*" and they push their children to fulfill their own dreams, even if that means the kids have to become different people in that pursuit.

But in all this, where does authenticity have space to grow in a child? I cannot but think of the several masks we are forced to wear in our lives, starting way early in school, where our grades decide what happens to us and the only way forward is to imbibe the qualities that the student with the top rank possesses, we were never just enough in of ourselves. Modeling ourselves to a successful pattern was our Darwinism, surviving and ensuring societal success is the journey and the goal. By now, we are far, far away from who we really are. While there were a couple of exceptional teachers, most were going through the motions. They probably did not like the job or just had way too much going on at their end. The only thing that mattered to them was that their classes did well overall so they looked good on the roster. The point is, we are often taught by teachers who do not relate to authenticity themselves. How could they teach us to be an authentic set of kids who knew ourselves inside out? That is the paradox in growing up. We create every possible condition for the child to not be who they are supposed to be. Something else is better. Who they are and what they are is passé: the human experience is about becoming better. Thus, we get on this 'better' treadmill that is perpetually on and we are stuck on it. It is designed such that it requires extraordinary will and perseverance to get off it, something that is hard to come by at that age.

We have also seen the rise of the social media and the interconnected culture which has incredible benefits but also encourages the human ego to put forth an exaggerated version of ourselves out there. We want to follow the trend, we have to – otherwise we would be left behind. But alas authenticity just kept getting pushed to the back row seats.

This is the success and the punishment of this generation. We have been successful in creating job warriors who will propel the economy forward by doing whatever it takes. With that we have created perfectly unique and healthy human beings who now find themselves sweating out long hours at a desk, and introduced them to obesity, depression, sleeping pills, creating a whole generation of young people who stare at their ceilings at night wondering where their life is going. There is inhibition around accepting our inability to find meaning and purpose in what we do. Remember the mask that still has not come off? The respite comes in small flashes of introspection where we recognize the incongruity or just feel the growing discomfort. That's when, even if just for a moment, we become an observer instead of a participant.

As I age, my appreciation and respect for authenticity has increased. The power of an authentic person is unmatched. A person may have no skills at all, but if they are in a room with their true authentic self, they stand out. They own the room. People get organically attracted to an authentic person. Creative people harness this power constantly.

In the summer of 2015, I attended a concert which was part of U2's Innocence and Experience tour. Our seats were pretty close to the stage and I could see Bono and the team up close. Although any superlatives on the experience of the concert will let the truth down, something else moved me beyond words. Bono was then 55 and had a smaller frame than I would have thought. From the first note he hit, he seemed to be possessed. He was possessed with a power to move mountains just as he moved the crowd. To witness and listen to his voice reverberating and piercing through the walls at the United Center in Chicago was pure magic. I just watched him, intently. Yes, it was years and years of practice. And yes, he was a master of his craft. But there was something more. He was channeling an internal power that was recognizable to each and every spirit present there. Using his body to aid this internal Godliness come through wholly and completely, not a second seemed like a real effort. I couldn't help but mutter the words, "He is just himself." Just an unadulterated form of being. And in that moment, I wondered if that is what happens when we reach complete congruence between our internal true self and our external body – a state of no effort that feels like pure magic. I was captured by a jealous feeling, in a not-so-negative way. I wanted to feel that, feel that so badly for myself. I remain in deep pursuit of this congruence when internal and external boundaries subside; when struggle and effort vanish.

The reason I am obsessed with my newborn son is that he is just wholly himself. There is no adulteration. Just like Bono when he is performing, his vicissitudes and idiosyncrasies are completely his. He doesn't know how to not be himself. Fortunately, he has not been handed any masks yet. I find myself watching him and hoping he never ever loses his own spark, uniqueness and chutzpah, that he always chooses his own self above being anyone else in any life situation. My hope and prayer for him is to know a life without any masks.

Takeaway

My hope and prayer for me and you in the journey is to reclaim our true selves, in spite of how our egos have evolved. Instead of trying to mold ourselves into who we think we should become, we listen to what life is saying to us and calling us to do. We embrace our limitations as much as our strengths – our 'wholeness of being.' I hope that not fitting into a successful job classification is not a matter of shame anymore – maybe it's just not who we are. My wish for the conscious parents is to nurture and protect their child's uniqueness fiercely. My prayer is that humanity learns to recognize and respect their true selves and let others just be. I can't wait to see the world in that state of congruency, where everyone is no one else but themselves. Who else could they be? I can only imagine miracles sparking everywhere!

Moment of contemplation:

What masks have you been compelled to wear since childhood? What circumstances from your teenage years contributed to creating those masks?

What purpose do these masks serve for you?

___

___

___

___

"Why are you so hard on yourself?"

"I am just not good enough, always making mistakes."

"Everyone makes mistakes."

"But I should not…"

Compassion for Thyself

"If your compassion does not include yourself, it is incomplete."

~Jack Kornfield

Dear P,

Do you know who was the hardest toward me growing up? No, it was not the guy who pelted stones at me every day for four years when I was on my way home from school just to get my attention; it was not the guy who put indecent letters in my school bag which were later found by my mom; it was not the guy who never returned my call after the first date. I was the hardest toward me – at all times. Every time.

I was 14 years old when a guy grabbed me by my neck in darkness and physically abused me, a few blocks from my house. I was coming back from my everyday swimming drills and never would I have guessed that day would change my life. For years, I blamed myself for the incident. I was ashamed of myself – for wearing a skirt that night, for coming back home at 7pm, for being a girl. To rectify it, I used all the remedies possible, like changing my clothing, not being out after about 6pm, feeling depressed, not talking to boys, all the while feeling disgusted with myself. But never did it cross my mind in those initial years that that son of a gun could have been at fault. Never.

It is so contradicting that being of service was my highest goal and empathy my highest quality. I could empathize with people who wouldn't respect my space and time, arguing for them to understand their insensitivity, but I could beat myself up for days for making a simple mistake.

To understand this phenomenon better, I went back to my childhood. Somewhere along the way, my parents developed perfect pictures for me. Perfect pictures are pictures of how we should be in every circumstance of life, the best way to behave. I demanded extremely high standards from myself, which meant I lived in a perpetual state of guilt because I was never enough. Faring well was always a normal thing – meh, not a big deal. But I could easily spend a couple of sleepless nights if I didn't go above and beyond on the homework. My expectations of myself were enormous. But I showed myself no mercy. I had immense compassion for others, but I lacked compassion for the most important person to me: me! I had to constantly do more to measure up.

Many moons later, I learnt the art of blowing up my perfect pictures I had gathered, mostly from my parents. There is nothing to blame our parents for. They did what they learnt and knew to be the best. It is so important to understand whose pictures you are carrying in your space – that best friend you had growing up, that aunt who relentlessly advised, a teacher who always resisted you – find out those impressions and who created them so you can focus on them intently with accuracy and release them. All I needed to do was to keep the intention, see the picture and visualize the blowing up of those pictures. I cried a bunch because I was letting go of years of pain of not meeting expectations and letting people down. But boy, was I relieved.

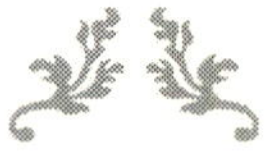

Takeaway

Yes, motivation and the drive to keep moving ahead is important. But as I understand now, it's equally important to pause and say, "I am enough" and "It's OK if I messed up," and for a change, give myself the benefit of the doubt. If we model our lives on others' expectations, we will never be enough. It always feels short and leaves room for so much more. Compassion for others is the highest virtue. But an even greater act would be to offer it to ourselves first and cut ourselves some slack! Service starts at our own abode. We can only give that which we have for ourselves.

Moment of contemplation:

When you make a mistake, what's your self-talk like?

Do you ever get a sense of, "*I need to do more andI need to be more*"? Go back to your childhood for a second. Who is this modeled after? Who in your family was never happy with what they had or achieved?

"I deserve better, far better."

"Why do you deserve better?"

"Because I worked hard."

"So…?"

Fallacy of Merit

"Everything you want is coming. Relax and let the universe pick up the timing and the way."

~Abraham Hicks

Dear P,

When we were growing up, cause and effect was primary education at home, in school and with friends. You take another spoon of baby food, you get some more entertainment from your mom. You behave yourself at the movies, you get a kiss and a hug from your dad. Do well in school, you get a prize. You always do something and you can expect to get something in return. But somewhere down the line, we rationalize that whenever we do something, we should always get what we deserve or, worse yet, what we want. There is much hoopla around merit and the philosophy of what we deserve. We imagine that commensurate to X amount of work, we should get Y. Now, Y can be based on many things – similar circumstances experienced by our friends or the world at large, our past experience doing X, the stories that mom used to tell when we were really young, or it could totally be a work of fiction!

Time and again, I have felt that I did not get the promotion I deserved or a raise that should have come to me much earlier, or that someone else in the office got what they did not deserve. But who decides what I deserve or someone does not deserve? And who am I to make that decision?

There is a hint of amusement within me when I hear myself or my friends talk about failures and successes and whether they were truly deserving or not. When we do a job, there is no balance in the world that can accurately calculate what we should get in return. I might study really hard and get the highest grades in my class. I got what I deserved ... right? But now consequently, I am now under pressure to perform every year and therefore I get into a hidden depression. Did I get what I deserve? What about a new mom nursing her newborn every hour through many nights. What does she deserve? What I am trying to say is when we look at an event, it is just one piece of the larger puzzle. Since our lives are a giant puzzle with interconnected pieces, we cannot look at a localized event and judge it to be rightly deserving or not. And this is sometimes beyond what we can comprehend.

There is a famous line in Hindi literature written by the famous Harivansh Rai Bacchan "*man ka ho toh aacha, man ka na ho toh jyada aacha.*" The translation is that when things pan out the way you'd like, then it's good, but when they don't, it may be even better. It took me a long time to understand the "even better" bit. And I struggled with this flaw in the prose for a while. I made up my mind that it was the loser's excuse or a way for us to feel better when we lose. But it's taken me 30 years to understand that life's canvas is so huge that it's hard to understand what effect a stroke of color on one end of our life has on another. That the universe is always at play and it always on our side, no matter how bad the present circumstances turn out to be.

Takeaway

When things don't go our way, there is a higher power in control to guide us intelligently and for us to get a better deal at the very end. Yes, there is temporary, sometimes even unbearable pain, but by trusting the universe and not falling for age-old ideas about merit, we may be happier. This is never easy to understand intellectually, but it starts making more sense as we make this understanding a way of life. This is an exploration of the depths of human consciousness and a fun activity as an observer of the mind.

Moment of contemplation:

What is your reaction to not getting something at work like a promotion or a raise?

How do you feel about surrendering the reins of life to the universe? Does that idea scare you?

"I have changed my job again."

"Do you feel a lot better now?"

"They all suck after some time."

Changing the Inside

"If you get the inside right, the outside will fall into place. Primary reality is within; secondary reality without."

~Eckhart Tolle

Dear P,

While I was growing up, there was my inner space, my thoughts, secrets and characters, while on the outside were my relationships with friends and family, my grades, my relationship with my teachers. Everything happening outside of me was disconnected from me, like it was happening to someone else. I was watching a movie and it was not relatable to my life and that left me feeling very isolated from the world during my teens.

I struggled with self-image issues through it all – I was too short, too wide, and way too dark. I had a list of flaws that I went through every day, reinforcing them every year that I existed on the planet. I soon realized that people around me, in my social circle and even people who I had just met responded in agreement with my flaws. They all validated my checklist. I tried to change my friends, my entire circle of people I hung out with, but that didn't change a thing about me or my ideas of myself. I'd made a huge assumption that changing my outside would fix everything in my life.

We could focus all our life on the outside: why did we develop the habits that we did? Why we have the wrong people around us all the time? Why we get into bad relationships or why we always find a job we don't like? It doesn't even occur to us that this could be a symptom of not having fixed something inside yet. That maybe, just maybe, once we ease out the inside and learn to love and respect ourselves, we might start getting the same from the outside. Our surrounding structures and relationships are a direct reflection of the happenings in our inside world.

I have gone through stages of exploring my relationship with my mother. It went from being strained to really important for my well-being. I realized that the only shift I needed was to surrender to the fact that she is her own woman. My need to change her came from a desire to control and be right always. I just needed to tone it down, add some humor and raise the energy a notch. And that changed our relationship. Changing my mother was not an option. The change had to start within me.

People go through multiple relationships complaining about how tough it is to find the right one. We don't look within us to change: we are looking for the other to be perfect. Yes, an outside change is easier to bring about, and it allows us to be the victim, which is the cherry on the top. There is something highly comforting but immensely disturbing about being a victim. That's what we do with our relationships – we keep changing them to solve a deeper discontent in our lives. When we realize we are energy and spirit, that we are God-like, that our bodies are mortal and hence circumstances and their consequences are fleeting, we don't feel the rush to change the outside as the first resort.

Who we present ourselves to be or what we do in the outside doesn't matter. It does not matter if you are a doctor, lawyer, environmentalist, glaciologist – it really does not. Suffering of all sorts will still come. Suffering doesn't say, "Oh, I see you are an engineer, let's not piss you off." I sort of thought it worked that way and thus I became one but alas … But I think suffering does look at a few things: *"Does she know who she is? What is her inner space like? Will it annihilate me through the strength of her presence?"*

Have you ever seen miraculous makeovers in people's lives? They lose 200lbs, turn around their life of addiction into something meaningful, or transform themselves from a couch potato into a marathon runner? This is rarely caused by outside events. It is brought upon by an inside shift, an internal transformation, the breaking of a hard shell that requires a certain resolve that we are capable of but most don't reach for.

My area of control ends at the edge of my aura. Nothing beyond that is under my control. I can influence change, but I don't control the change. Surrender has worked for me in most situations as the one shift that manifested in a plethora of external changes. Yes, it's difficult and yes, it takes time. As I look back on the past two decades of my life, there are only handful of internal changes that have been established. But what is mind-blowing is the number of changes in my circle of experience these handful of changes have brought upon. You don't need many to really transform our lives.

Takeaway

You may need to change a job, a relationship or yank yourselves out of a messy situation but do it consciously with presence, not with unconscious energies of rage, anger, guilt, blame, etc. But every time you feel the urge to change something outside, do a self-check. It's time to go to the wise one within and ask a few questions. "*What am I fearful of? What am I running away from? What is that one thing I can change in me that can turn this situation around?*" We get our answers within and we address it within. I no longer have to change my job, my house, my car, my relationship, my school, my parents, my friends … most of the time! More often than not, a shift within renders an outside change useless and unnecessary.

Moment of contemplation:

Describe one situation in your life that you want to change.

What change can you bring about in your life right now that can help manage this situation better?

"Ahh, these big questions!"

"What about them?"

"They don't leave me alone."

We Might Never Figure it Out

"The voyage of discovery is not in seeking new landscapes but in having new eyes."

~Marcel Proust

Dear P,

Loner. Thinker. Pensive. These words got attached to me organically while growing up. I liked to think about life and make sense of my space. In my early 20s, the purpose of why I am here was all I could think about. I pondered and then some. Life was a mystery. But I was also aware of how engrossed I was in the minutiae of life – homework, conflict at school and home, finding my identity developing my arsenal of fears. Life was full.

But then I had some rare moments when I could step back and look back at times past. Look at my 15, 19, 27 year old selves. Conclusion – I had never stopped worrying about my circumstances in life: it was either worrying about the now, the future or just all of it. I was trying hard, very hard, to figure life out. And the harder I thought, the harder it got. But the good news in all of this were the nuggets of life I kept capturing all along.

Here, let me burst the bubble for you. You no longer have to wonder if life is confusing. It is! There are no two ways about it, really. One moment you feel like it would be great if the Earth cracked open and you disappeared into it. Other times, your heart fills up with so much joy that tears well up. On one hand, you believe in going with the flow, and then on the other, you finally look for a purpose in life, which should have been found yesterday! Life never gets less bewildering. There are moments, sometimes a nanosecond (whoever knows how long that is!), where we feel calm, peaceful and happy. Questions subside for a fair second and we have a feeling that life is, well, figured out. But then the next second, we are back with our questions, thoughts, fears and expectations.

I have heard of saints, gurus and swamis attaining enlightenment. I have not been hit by that bus yet, so I cannot speak to it except that those very short glimpses have been extremely powerful. Now, it's fairly possible that I attain that level of enlightenment and in that state of being, I either get all my answers in a moment or I don't need answers to them anymore – I think they are the same thing anyway. It is also fairly possible that I never find out what this journey was all about; that I live until the end of my life with the big questions in my heart.

I may never figure it out. My answers may keep changing with different phases of my life as I am graced by richer experiences, and there may be days when I am utterly confused by all my answers. But I believe that this confusion is not a failure but a success of life. Curiosity is the bloodline of a rich life. Life will evolve and so will the answers and the best course for me is to stay an observer of my answers and trust the answers for what they are at that stage. The right answer is the one we get at the time when we really need it. May be there is no right answer and I may never get THE answer until the end of life. There might not even be one. I need to be OK with that uncertainty. I need to be OK with not knowing the ultimate.

I just may never figure all this out. But I will keep asking the questions and listening to my answers. Neale Donald Walsch said a line that I truly love: "Life will figure out in the process of life itself." It seemed counter-intuitive to me when I first heard it. I thought we were supposed to work it, work life until it finally starts to figure itself out. That we the humans are driving life and it's not the other way around. I had romanticized the idea that losing ourselves in the mysterious journey of life and then trying really hard to find the right path was what this game was all about. But after getting lost for several years, and then finding my way and then losing myself again, I think it's a way more fun to let life play it out. Give it the chance to flow its natural way. Can we take the chance of not rowing for a change and just float in the oarless boat?

This is what I know: the questions and the answers live within us. Enlightenment is within us. Seeking is a journey and an endeavor to create the silence that holds space to the answers we are curious about. As we honor this process, we honor the answers that arise and the ones that don't.

Takeaway

We will probably never figure out the answer to the life's big questions. *What is the purpose of life? What is life all about? Who am I? Why am I here?* But what if we give life the chance to blossom the answers at the right time, in the process of life itself? The answer that is right for us. The answer that lives in our experience. What if, as we move from moment to moment, with our presence intact, we come to realize who we are and why we are here? Maybe it's just a glimpse, maybe it stays. As much as I love to analyze life and write about it, there is a sort of liberation in letting it all go. Let life make sense of itself and show itself to me in due time. And I realize that the only way I can be a witness to that is if I am present across all moments. Do I think I will live each moment with great peace and a feeling of immense joy – nah, probably not going to happen! And that's OK. As long as I know that life's experiences are working their wheels to get me to my next great adventure and it's going to figure itself out, all I need to do is to just consciously breathe.

Moment of contemplation:

What are the big questions you are seeking answers to?

What if you do not get answers by the end of this life? How will that make you feel?

____

____

____

____

"Death seems dangerous and mysterious."

"Do you feel there is anything that death can teach you?"

"Death … it seems so far-fetched."

Death as the Highest Teacher

"Don't be afraid of death; be afraid of an unlived life. You don't have to live forever; you just have to live."

~Natalie Babbitt

Dear P,

There is a lot going on in the world. Suddenly, my mortality gapes at me more intently than ever before. Very rarely have we been so vulnerable to the prospect of dying due to external reasons in the most common of situations. I no longer have to be in a battle zone to lose my life. I realize I can die shopping for watermelons in the neighborhood grocery store, while running on the lakeshore, at the local café while eating my croissant or while giving a presentation at work.

Grateful is not a word we would use for the incidents in motion across the world. But I am grateful for the realization that death is imminent. The knock on the door is hard, calling us to take notice of our whole lives – on how we are living, on the definitions of success we have long harbored or the enormous amount of un-forgiveness that hides within us.

Death can be the greatest teacher, as in the face of it, every semblance of urgent and important that we have long held dear, weathers away. We stand face-to-face with what is real. *Are these traumatic incidents across the world here to remind us to take notice? Are they here to remind us to 'die' that self that is no longer working, before we die?*

I rejoice in the fact that the inevitability of death has forced me to think about some important questions that have been waiting to be asked for a while. I know I no longer have eternity to get to them. The faster I can confront the questions and befriend the answers, the better off I am to fully experience my lifetime. Here are some key questions that death encourages me to consider as it becomes more of a reality with every passing day.

Are we all connected? Our bubble of life consists of the relationships that we came with or have made here, our jobs, the chores and our thoughts and emotions about our life. The incidents around the world are calling us to burst the bubble we are in and recognize how interconnected our lives truly are. We are hurt when a dead Syrian child is found in the shores of Turkey and we feel angst when innocent people are killed mercilessly, no matter where they are in the world. We are all part of a connected consciousness which is affected by the awakening of each and every one of us. Every time we love, forgive, accept, serve, we impact the world and raise its vibration. We may or may not be able to solve terrorism in the years to come, but the so-called terrorists are also a part of the unified consciousness, whether they like it or not. We don't have to take up guns, carry rage or go on a public demonstration. Love is the highest vibration there is. With love comes acceptance and forgiveness. Can we bring more of that into our lives? Each and every one of us has a role to play in creating a better world for our children, nieces, nephews and grandchildren. Let's get on with it.

Is that success? We are neither rich nor successful when death is up close. We are a body and a soul, striving to stay intact for some more. We are a husband, father, mother, wife, daughter or son. We are mentors, coaches, confidantes and friends. We are the life of every party. We are compassionate, enthusiastic, exuberant and sensitive. Let's reflect on the importance we give to money, image and the corporate ladder. Walker Percy wrote, "You can get all As and still flunk life. *"Would we have flunked life at the end of our lives?"*

Can I forgive? We carry un-forgiveness in our hearts for long forgotten incidents, sometimes for people we love dearly. Not only do we prevent a beautiful relationship from being part of our life, the unsaid heaviness in our hearts poisons us relentlessly from within. Most of the time it's our ego that wants to continue the drama. It would be so easy to let go with a mere, "Sorry, let's move on," but we don't. We are also incredibly unforgiving of our own selves – for the mistakes we made a long time ago or when we did not know better. Looking at life through 'no-forgiveness' glasses, towards others or our own selves is no fun. At the end moment of our life, I wonder if our grudges make it onto the important list. Maybe we realize that the pedestal we held ourselves on didn't really mean anything.

How can I be of service? When we serve, we align with the raw version of our self, the self we spend a lot of time and money awakening otherwise. We don't have to open a charity or serve in one to be of service. Service can begin in our homes, our neighborhood and community. Due to the interconnectedness of humanity, service done in our own backyard heals the whole world. No service goes unnoticed in the tapestry of life and beyond.

What am I called to do? We are all here to give something to the world. We are called to realize our purpose. But the thought agitates many, as it challenges the status quo of our lives. We would rather be busy than divine. Our calling keeps nudging us (in ways that we are very aware of), but we ignore and banish it till the nudges fade. As we connect to the things that are fervently calling us, we honor the divinity of all life. People connected to their purpose are connected to an inner reservoir of calm that touches each and every one they meet. It's not just about you or me, our connection to our calling impacts every human touch point.

Am I grateful? We as humans are a privileged lot. For all our hardships of living in a world caught up in thoughts and emotions, we live amidst incredible beauty. Whether it is the mesmerizing sunrise every day or feeling the compassion and unconditional love of a mother, the rainbow is always there to notice and cherish when we are not caught up in a particular band of the spectrum. We feel what we feel because of our human form. And it may be a funny potpourri, but it is undeniably interesting and if seen closely, pretty mind-blowing. We will forever not have enough to feed our ego, but what we have today is great and worth admiring. We get to live another day, to breathe the air, to feel the breeze, to feel the sunlight fall on our face and to love and be loved. How can we not say ... thank you.

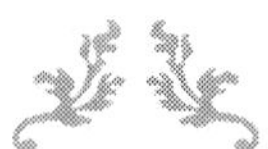

Takeaway

We don't need to ponder on death. Just keeping the awareness of our mortality at decisive times in our lives can serve as a determining pointer. When all else fails, the awareness of our impermanence can stand up strong against the most tiresome and annoying ego battles within us and with others.

Moment of contemplation:

What do you think about your own mortality?

What do you think would cross your mind if death was close?

"What is the purpose of your life?"

"I have no idea. I just have a nagging feeling there is probably one out there."

The Burden of Purpose

"What if God forgot to give you a purpose? What if there is no purpose?"

~Sadhguru

Dear P,

I want to talk about something that has taken so much of my head-space for a fairly long time. You will be introduced to a concept in your early twenties that will strike you like a thunderstorm, crack you open with a jolt and leave you with this simple question: "*What is your purpose in life?*" And it will consume every cell of your being. I spent years tossing and turning at night, waking up at 3:47AM every day for months and wondering if I was supposed to work on my unknown purpose at this hour. I am in my 30s now and there are days when I am completely taken by the burden of this question. Apart from my husband, this unresolved question is the longest-running relationship of my life. There is no respite from knowing that life is more than a quarter over and there is a higher calling for me which I just cannot seem to find. There is nothing more frustrating than knowing that I may not be on the path that I am meant to be on.

But here is the weird thing: life did not come with a manual which said, "Here, now go find your purpose". What if, just what if, we have been thinking of purpose very prescriptively? *Are we seeking purpose in vain? Is life, this life, the real true purpose? Do we need to have a higher purpose than just being the life-force we are?* Maybe, maybe not. I don't know the answer. All I know is that a lot of us are reeling under the pressure of a potentially divine purpose. It's a frustrating question, because our education, societal and parental systems are far from ready to answer these questions or guide us with pointers. I did not enjoy my youth because I was looking for something that the whole universe seemed to be asking me to find. I was so consumed by the concept that the everyday beauty of life was just lost in me. I couldn't see the present because the purpose was always in the future and I had to find it.

Later in my 20s, I was surprised by a beautiful and welcome insight about how nature behaves which gave me an understanding of the nature of life itself. I observed the trees, the leaves, the branches, the lone flower in the middle of the bush and the bush itself. For once, I really looked at them without giving them a name or judging them on any of their characteristics. *Why do I think they exist?* They just exist, exist some more and then pass on. Everything in nature seems to … just be. A tree seems to have no other inward purpose but to flow with nature, in complete acceptance of its appearance, its location or type. Its outward purpose of being a shade, a spiritual pad, or a pointer to spiritual seekers, comes later as a result of the tree's complete harmony with its presence. Look at the beauty of a flower – does it get to score more points for its color or the number of petals it has? I guess not. Flowers exist with complete acceptance and surrender to something bigger than themselves. They are as accepting in life as they will be at the time of their death. *Is it possible that my purpose in life is no different than the trees or the ocean? Is it possible that my purpose is to just Be?* I may or may not land on my so-called purpose in life. But I sure as hell won't get back those days I spent in despair searching for that elusive goal.

On a beautiful fall night while driving back home, I offered up my face to the chilly winds under a full moon. In that moment, I realized why I am in a physical body, why I exist. I also understood that this was a fleeting realization and that this would not stay with me forever. But in that moment, I did not have any questions about my purpose. I was life. I have no better knowledge of life and its intricacies than anyone else. None of us have been handed the manual to operate. We learn to drive, make some mistakes and drive some more. I write about what I experience. I write what life teaches me, as I live through it every day. And so far life has been really wishy-washy on the question of purpose. And I think that's deliberate. That's the only way we can keep our curiosity intact for all things joyous to us.

Takeaway

If you stumble on the question of purpose, know that where you will eventually land on after much ado is that *the highest of all purpose is life itself.* We are alive, so many are not. We are fulfilling our purpose by being the life-force that we are, and we can only be that by enjoying what we have right in front of us. Honoring life this way may lead you to experiences or vocations that you feel inclined to take on as you continue to be curious about the elements of life. There may not be anything grandiose about your life through your eyes, but LIFE itself is grandiose. We lose sight of what this life grants us every day as the sun shines – possibilities, dreams, and the human potential to make our dreams come true, and the gamut of beautiful experiences of love, kindness, gratitude. Ahhh. So much. This is grandiose. This is purpose. Amen.

Moment of contemplation:

Do you ever wonder what the purpose of your life is?

How would you feel if I told you that living is our purpose? How do you feel about that? Does that cause any disappointment in you?

____

____

____

____

"Sometimes, I just know that I need to return home."

"Where is home?"

"Right here."

The Road to Completion

"When Essence becomes Expression, and Expression becomes Experience, The Totality of You has known Divinity."

~Neale Donald Walsh

Dear P,

I am going to keep this one short. Through these notes to you, I have played with many different emotions that I have experienced in more than 30 years of life. If I have to round out the whole gig called life, here it is: *All I ever wanted to do was to express who I truly am, sometimes successfully, but mostly in pursuit.*

I was looking for that thing that would complete me. I looked for books, friends, jobs, lovers, parents and vacations to do the job. I was knocking on all of these doors just to find 'that' thing. Yes, it is hard to find. But as I have learnt, completion is not an external phenomenon, as we are either led to believe or we somehow deduce. It is a purely internal event. I also think it's not a big kaboom! We can experience multiple completion points in our life. Every time we express that truth of who we are now and we live that experience fully, we are complete.

That restlessness, that feeling of hollowness, discontent – it's all the desire to reach completion, which is the intersection point of body, mind and soul. That's where peace and an indelible contentment resides. It's not boastful, it's a humble "*Ahhh.*" It's not saying, "*You have now arrived.*" It's saying, "*Hello, friend, you belong and I see you now.*"

I reckon that's why nothing forced can ever lead to completion. That job that I am just doing, or the book that I am writing because I have to write it, the art that is not driven by an invisible power that moves our hands – these can try to create a semblance of completion, but that's the extent of it. They just leave us seeking more. Our power to create anything great is not ours at all, it's only when we connect with our essence in great stillness that we find the special something that has the power to create things that will resonate with beings all across the universe. If it doesn't come from essence, it comes from ego. And ego only creates a constant sense of never having enough. Nothing spectacular has ever come out of that.

The beauty of this journey is that to realize our completion, we have to be ok with the feeling of being incomplete; because this surrendering creates space for our essence to rise.

But here is the twist I am going to leave you with…

I think we are already complete. I believe the road to completion is just the path to remembering just that. The feeling of discontent and restlessness is begging us to remember that there is nothing else we need, other than to own the truth of our essence. We are complete when we realize through our own experience that we are indeed already there.

All of life comes to a simple equation: *Express your essence and experience that which results.* That's what we are all looking for.

Onward…

One Last Thought…

I will end with where we started. *Are you indeed restless?* Then pay attention. Observe your life, one breath at a time. Something happens when we pay attention to the life force inside us, instead of the myriad things and thoughts around. Talk, sing, paint, write, blog, or vlog about it. The source within us wants to express itself. Open up the clogs in the drain and let it all out. I just did …

Made in the USA
Middletown, DE
26 March 2019